A CHRISTIAN'S POCKET GUIDE TO

BAPTISM

Here is a robust, articulate and biblical presentation of covenant baptism that avoids populism and individualism. Dr Letham has placed baptism in its covenantal and canonical context – a work of God rather than an act of obedience – no bare sign but an active means of grace – for believers and their children. Drawing from the totality of divine revelation rather than a few isolated proof texts, baptism is seen in historical continuity with its OT roots, its relationship to the covenant of grace in its various administrations, and in its practical implications for Christian living.

LIAM GOLIGHER,
Senior Minister, Tenth Presbyterian Church,
Philadelphia, Pennsylvania

Rightly does Letham seek to understand the issue of baptism within the canonical framework of Scripture. He is hopeful that this is the way forward beyond the impasse that has stymied the church for centuries regarding this precious ordinance. While I agree wholeheartedly with this approach and believe that an excellent case for the paedobaptist position has been made by Letham, I remain fundamentally unconvinced by his argument, being assured that the new covenant contains a newness only satisfactorily explained by Baptists. But if you are searching for a well-argued, and irenic, approach to this subject from the vantage-point of infant baptism, this is the book for you.

MICHAEL A.G. HAYKIN
Professor of Church History and Biblical Spirituality,
The Southern Baptist Theological Seminary, Louisville, Kentucky

A CHRISTIAN'S POCKET GUIDE TO

BAPTISM

THE WATER THAT UNITES

ROBERT LETHAM

CHRISTIAN
FOCUS

Copyright © Robert Letham 2012

ISBN 978-1-84550-968-2

10 9 8 7 6 5 4 3 2 1

Published in 2012
by
Christian Focus Publications Ltd,
Geanies House, Fearn, Ross-shire,
IV20 1TW, Scotland, Great Britain

www.christianfocus.com

Cover design by Paul Lewis

Printed by Nørhaven, Denmark

All rights reserved. No part of this publication may be reproduced, stored in a retrieval system, or transmitted, in any form, by any means, electronic, mechanical, photocopying, recording or otherwise without the prior permission of the publisher or a licence permitting restricted copying. In the U.K. such licences are issued by the Copyright Licensing Agency, Saffron House, 6-10 Kirby Street, London, EC1 8TS www.cla.co.uk.

CONTENTS

ACKNOWLEDGEMENTS

It is my happy task to thank those who have contributed in various ways towards the production of this book. On a visit to Wales, accompanied by his wife, William Mackenzie of Christian Focus Publications asked me to produce a small book on baptism. I agreed readily since I had given the matter much thought over the years. I am thankful for his giving me the opportunity to do so. Philip Ross has been extremely helpful in his comments on the manuscript. I am also grateful to a number of friends and colleagues who have read the draft and made suggestions, many of which have vastly improved the finished article. It goes without saying that not all of them will agree with everything written here but each one has been very gracious and their help is deeply appreciated. These include The Rev. Jonathan Stephen, Principal, Wales Evangelical School of Theology and a pastor for nearly thirty years, formerly Senior Minister of Carey Baptist Church, Reading; my colleague The Rev. Dr Tom Holland, a distinguished New Testament scholar and former pastor and church planter of thirty-five years' experience; Dr Natalie Brand, theologian and pastor's wife; and my friend The Rev. Lee F. Veazey, Minister of Grace and Peace Presbyterian Church (PCA), Covington, Kentucky. None can be charged with any errors in the book; the views expressed are my own. As always, I give thanks for my wife, Joan, whose constant support is an inspiration.

My hope and prayer is that we may all come to a greater appreciation of baptism and all that it signifies, growing in union with Christ and one another in his church, and that there may be a renewed and widespread consideration for the biblical teaching on the status and nurture of the children of believers, and to its faithful implementation.

PART ONE

FOUNDATIONAL PRINCIPLES

Baptism is a matter often fraught with discord and strife. One popular book described it as 'the water that divides.'[1] This is a tragedy, since it is the sign of our union with Christ and his church. It should be a focus for union rather than division. Yet I have known many people who have been excluded from church membership and ministry because their baptism was not held to conform to what was regarded as biblical. How can this division be overcome? Is this a simple matter, to be resolved if only everyone were to submit to the plain and obvious teaching of the Bible? Or are deeper questions involved?

When we disagree on biblical teaching it is important that we consider factors affecting the way we interpret the Bible, and so shape our understanding of doctrine. Our reading of Scripture is often governed by unconscious principles that influence what we can see in the text. Elsewhere I have argued that we can study the Bible until we are blue in the face but we will never come to an agreement on disputed questions such as whether infants are to be baptized until we have uncovered these factors.[2] Only then will we appreciate what drove the biblical authors and the church down the ages in its interpretation of the Bible. A key to reading a book of the Bible—or any document, for that matter—is for us to determine, as far as we can, what was the intention of the person who wrote it. Often our own cultural and philosophical assumptions can hamper this process. In this first section, we will ask how far our reading of Scripture is to be taken into account in understanding what baptism means and who should receive it.

We will also argue that not only the surface text of Scripture but its implications and entailments are part of its overall teaching. The church fathers constantly appealed to 'the rule of faith' in their preaching and teaching. By this they were maintaining that the way we read the Bible must always be checked against the central truths of the Christian faith. Moreover, since the Bible consists of two sections, integrally connected, we need to read it as a whole, canonically. This means that we need to grasp what baptism is and signifies against the background of the history of salvation as it unfolds in Old Testament and New Testament.

Again, since God created the entire universe, our salvation embraces matter as well as spirit. Consequently, the sacraments God has appointed—baptism and the Lord's Supper in the New Testament—must not be dismissed as of only incidental significance in the

Christian life but should be seen as integral to the way God ministers his grace to his church.

Finally in this first section we will examine the relationship between the individual and the corporate as it appears in both Testaments. In the Western world, we are accustomed to viewing ourselves as individuals. In the world of the Bible, people thought rather differently than we do. This issue affects the question of how we view the family, the household, and consequently children. The conclusions we draw will affect who we baptize. So these foundational principles are vital to grasp, since they often govern the way we read the Bible, understand its teaching and implement it in practice.

⚠ Warning
📎 Don't Forget
⑦ Stop and Think
✹ Point of Interest

1

INTERPRETING THE BIBLE:

THE TEXT AND ITS IMPLICATIONS

Many Christians are convinced that all we need to do is to open our Bibles and the answers will spring ready-made from the text. The truth is not entirely like that. The teaching of Scripture is rich and multi-layered and is found in two distinct, but inseparable, ways. There are explicit statements on particular matters. These are fairly clear, if taken in context. The gospel itself is presented like this in many places. John tells us that 'God loved the world in this way, that he gave his only-begotten Son, so that whoever believes in him should not perish but have everlasting life' (John 3:16). There are many similar statements in the Bible on a range of matters that are clear and decisive in themselves.

However, as one great Protestant confession put it, the whole counsel of God for his glory, man's salvation, faith and life is not only expressly set down in Scripture but also 'by good and necessary consequence may be deduced from Scripture.' (*Westminster Confession of Faith* [*WCF*] 1:6).[3] This is due to there being many things in the Bible that are hard to understand. Even the apostle Peter found the letters of Paul at times beyond his mental capacities (2 Pet. 3:16). Hence, prolonged thought and reflection is needed.[4] For instance, the overall teaching of the Bible is held by the church down the centuries to give overwhelming voice to the fact that the one God exists indivisibly as the Father, the Son, and the Holy Spirit. However, no one sentence states it in so many words.

It may be a surprise that until the eighteenth-century Enlightenment, many heresies arose from the demand for exact support from explicit biblical statements. The trinitarian crisis of the fourth century is a leading example. Followers of Eunomius, a bishop who championed ideas similar to those of the earlier heretic Arius, demanded that the defenders of the doctrine of the trinity produce chapter and verse from the Bible to prove it. Arius and Eunomius both claimed that the Son, while creator, was himself created. He was a different being than God. Nowhere in Scripture was it said in so many words that he was one with the Father from eternity, they claimed. Arians, Eunomians, and Macedonians all appealed to Scripture, contending that the orthodox used unscriptural terms.[5] Gregory of Nazianzus, in defending the doctrine of the trinity, replied 'Over and over again you turn upon us the silence of Scripture.' He pointed out that the Fathers, on the other hand, in their handling of the Bible, 'have gone beneath the letter and looked into the inner meaning.'[6] Instead, the heretics' 'love for the letter is but a cloak for their impiety.'[7] Scripture uses metaphors and figures of speech. Slavery to a literal interpretation, Gregory said, is an erroneous exegetical and theological method.[8] Ironically, the heretics favourite terms for God, 'unbegotten' and 'unoriginate' were not in the Bible at all.[9]

Closer to our day, B.B. Warfield remarked: 'The re-emergence in recent controversies of the plea that the authority of Scripture is to be confined to its express declarations, and that human logic is not to be trusted in divine things, is, therefore, a direct denial of a fundamental position of Reformed theology, explicitly affirmed in the Confession, as well as an abnegation of fundamental reason, which would not only render thinking in a system impossible, but would discredit at a stroke many of the fundamentals of the faith, such e.g. as the doctrine of the Trinity, and would logically involve the denial of the authority of all doctrine whatsoever, since no single doctrine of whatever simplicity can be ascertained from Scripture except by the use of the process of the understanding.'[10] Warfield's point is vital. The church has the responsibility of thinking hard about the connections and entailments of the statements in the Bible.

A classic example of where biblical fundamentalism proved deadly is the case of the Jehovah's Witnesses. They despised the pronouncements of the great ecumenical councils of the church, particularly the first councils of Nicaea (325 AD) and Constantinople (381 AD) which resolved the trinitarian crisis and expounded the church's teaching on the trinity. Instead, the group preferred their own understanding of the Bible to the distillation of the biblical exegesis of the church expressed at both councils and confessed down the centuries. They started a journal, *Studies in the Scriptures*. What a fine sounding title! In reality it was designed to oppose the biblical profession of the Christian church over nearly two thousand years. In contrast to sects such as this, we must submit our biblical exegesis to that of others in the church (Eph. 5:21).

In short, in considering baptism—its nature and subjects—we need to think together the implications, entailments, and connections of a wide swathe of biblical truth. To what does this passage refer? How can we understand it in the historical and theological context of the book in which it occurs? How does it relate to other aspects of biblical revelation? This is to discern 'the sense of Scripture' as Gregory called it. Moreover, as with any topic we ought to ask what is the sense of the whole of Scripture, not merely an isolated text or a few passages here or there.

 When thinking about baptism we should deal not only with the express statements of the Bible but also with the wider sense of Scripture that is entailed in these pronouncements.

2

INTERPRETING THE BIBLE:

THE OLD AND THE NEW

It is something of a truism that we have two Testaments but one Bible. This was an issue fought out in the second century when the church condemned Marcion's rejection of the Old Testament as heretical. He held that the Old Testament portrayed a different 'god' than the god of the New Testament. The Old Testament deity— or demiurge—was the creator, a god of justice, law and wrath, fickle and cruel. The god revealed in the New Testament by Jesus was loving and gracious. Law was absolutely excluded. The most faithful exponent of this god was Paul together with his friend and colleague, Luke. So, for Marcion, the Old Testament was to be rejected, most of the New Testament was also suspect, while only the letters of Paul and, to a lesser extent, the compositions of Luke accurately reflected the truth.

The popularity of Marcion and his teachings forced the church to respond. His denigration of the Old Testament, and with it, the severance of creation and redemption seen in his proposition that there were two 'gods,' enabled the church to define the canon it had already received. The church recognized that the one God had a plan for our salvation that encompassed the whole of human history, from Adam to Abraham, Moses, and David, finding its fulfilment in the coming of the Son of God in Jesus Christ. Irenaeus, Tertullian and others were responsible for defending the faith against Marcion. It was clear to them, and to the church, that the Old Testament and New Testament stood together.[11] While there are elements of discontinuity between the two Testaments—and, above all, the New Testament is the fulfilment of what was pre-figured in the Old Testament—these must be seen in the context of their continuity.

GRACE—CONCEALED AND REVEALED

'Grace, concealed in the Old Testament, is revealed in the New,' wrote Augustine (*On the Spirit and the Letter*, 27). Entailed in this conclusion is the vital point that we cannot understand either Old Testament or New Testament aright in isolation from the other. Jesus' own method of biblical interpretation was to see all parts of

Scripture—the Old Testament as we now have it—as referring ultimately to himself. In Luke 24, following his resurrection, he explained to the disciples on the road to Emmaus that the law, the prophets and the psalms all spoke of him (Luke 24:25–7). Later that same day, to a larger gathering, he declared that all sections of the Old Testament referred to his sufferings and glory, and to the task of the church in preaching the gospel (Luke 24:44–7).

To appreciate the meaning of the New Testament, it is indispensable to have a grasp of the Old Testament. Matthew wrote his gospel to establish that Jesus is 'the son of David, the son of Abraham' (Matt. 1:1) and so the inheritor of the promises of the Abrahamic and Davidic covenants. He reinforces his history by indicating that Jesus fulfilled what was written in the Old Testament (Matt. 1:23, 2:5–6, 15, 23, 3:15, 5:17–20). The entire scope of his gospel is that the kingdom of God has now come and has extended to all nations, fulfilling the eschatological expectation of the Abrahamic covenant and so of the entirety of Israel's covenant history (Matt. 28:18–20).

The Letter to the Hebrews is virtually incomprehensible apart from an understanding of the history of Israel, particularly the priestly system of Leviticus. The author argues that Christ is superior to the prophets, the angels, Moses, Aaron and the Levitical priests; he is our great high priest who has decisively completed the saving plan of God foreshadowed in the Old Testament.

The Book of Revelation is saturated in Old Testament imagery. Virtually every comment, every detail in the many visions, relates to some place in the Old Testament. Christ, who now in his ascended glory is the ruler of kings on earth (Rev. 1:5), completes the whole tapestry of Old Testament prophecy and apocalyptic imagery.

THE NEW COVENANT FULFILS
THE ABRAHAMIC COVENANT

Central to this whole sweep of redemptive history is God's covenant. Made with Abraham, Isaac and Jacob, Yahweh renewed his covenantal commitment to their descendants at Sinai. Later, Jeremiah foretold that he was to make a new covenant (Jer. 31:31–33), bringing to fulfilment the Abrahamic covenant and his promise to Adam, writing his law on human hearts, and making effective and definitive atonement for sins.

This new covenant fulfils the covenants of the Old Testament, and is not a replacement. The *protevangelium* (the first announcement of the gospel) in Genesis 3:15 was fulfilled by Christ's conquest of the devil. There God promised Eve that one of her offspring would deal a deathly blow to the serpent and his offspring. Jesus announced that this had taken place (John 12:31–2).

The new covenant fulfils the central promise of the Abrahamic covenant, in which God promised that the offspring of Abraham would be the means of worldwide blessing. Paul argues that justification by faith applied to Abraham and David as well as to us (Rom. 4:1–8). Abraham looked forward to the time when the covenantal promise God had made would be realized; this has happened now that Christ has come (Rom. 4:9–25, Gal. 3:6–18), for he is the offspring in whom all the nations are blessed (Gen. 12:1–3, Matt. 28:18–20).

The *Westminster Confession of Faith* affirms that the Mosaic covenant was an administration of the one covenant of grace.[12] Paul states that the law, given at Sinai, was not contrary to the gracious purposes of God in the Abrahamic covenant. It supplemented that covenant but did not replace it. 'It was added because of transgressions until the seed should come to whom the promise had been made' (Gal. 3:19). Since it was added, the original covenant remained in force; an addition is supplementary. The Mosaic covenant did not undermine the promise to Abraham in any way. It never propounded a different way of salvation, for that was utterly impossible after the fall; from that point on the whole world was guilty before God. Indeed, the Mosaic covenant pre-eminently displayed the grace exhibited in the Abrahamic covenant. Its provision for the forgiveness of sins was strikingly evident in the sacrificial system. At the moment the covenant was enacted, the people of Israel stampeded into idolatry (Exod. 32:1–35); if the covenant were a strictly legal one Israel would have been cast off right away. No, on virtually every page grace is evident in the midst of the legal cast of the Sinai administration. Yahweh's forbearance with the repeated sins and apostasy of Israel and Judah is unmistakeable. The goal of that covenant was to lead the covenant people of God to their maturity with the coming of the promised mediator, foreshadowed in the sacrifices and ceremonies of the Mosaic cult. That mediator was the seed, the offspring, promised earlier to Abraham.

This continuity is nowhere more evident than in the new covenant, which entailed the writing of God's laws on the heart instead of merely externally on stone tablets. Under Moses the law stood outside the covenant members; in the new covenant the law is written on the heart by the Holy Spirit (Jer. 31:31–3). The substance of the covenant is the same; its administration differs. Throughout grace is dominant, constituting God's covenants after the fall, while the law regulates them. While there are obvious differences between the Mosaic covenant, established by Yahweh with Israel at Mount Sinai, and the new covenant instituted by Christ in the New Testament, there is also a prevailing continuity. As *The Westminster Confession of Faith* and the *1689 Baptist Confession* describe it, the covenant of grace has a unity in both Testaments, while its administration differs.[13]

In 2 Corinthians 3:6-11 Paul compares his ministry with that of Moses, asserting that he is a second Moses. Paul's ministry is superior to Moses' since it achieves what Moses could not do. The latter was a purely external ministry, whereas Paul's effects change. However, the underlying continuity is obvious. While Paul's ministry is with surpassing glory, both are glorious. With Paul, the Holy Spirit writes the law of God on the heart, rather than on stone tablets, but the same law is in view. Again, the contrast in Hebrews 8:6–13—where the Mosaic economy is seen as old and obsolete, about to be abolished—must be seen in the context of the relationship between shadow (the Mosaic economy) and fulfilment (Christ).[14]

THE NEW COVENANT
IS SEALED IN CHRIST'S BLOOD

Christ took Adam's place, fulfilling the covenant of life which Adam had broken. Whereas Adam, tempted in a beautiful garden, succumbed to sin, the second Adam, tempted in a barren desert, remained faithful. Adam sinned in connection with a tree; the last Adam made atonement on the tree. Christ's atoning death, the shedding of his blood on the cross, atones emphatically, once-for-all, for all our sins. This fulfils the words of the prophet Micah, insofar as God has buried our sins in the depths of the sea (Mic. 7:18–20). Correspondingly, Christ's resurrection achieves our justification, received through faith. It was his vindication before the entire cosmos; in union with him we are justified in his resurrection (Rom. 4:25).[15] Furthermore, since all he is and all he does is in union with us, his ascension puts us in the heavenly places, with him in the presence of the Father (Eph. 2:4–7). The significance of this is that baptism is into the new covenant name of the Father, the Son, and the Holy Spirit (Matt. 28:18–20).[16]

A CANONICAL APPROACH TO BAPTISM

When we discuss baptism, we need to adopt a canonical perspective, taking into view the whole Bible. Baptism was instituted as a covenant sign in the New Testament but its meaning and significance cannot be established from the New Testament alone. As the Bible is a whole, and the New Testament cannot be read aright in isolation from the Old Testament, so the new covenant is rooted in the history of salvation stretching back to the early chapters of Genesis, and its signs express its identity as the fulfilment of God's promises expressed in covenant history. Baptism, as the sign of initiation into the new covenant, cannot be understood aright if it is treated in detachment from the history and fulfilment of the covenant with which it is connected. Just as the new covenant must be seen against the backcloth of the development of Yahweh's covenantal purposes with his people in the Old Testament, so must we understand baptism in a similar way.

Consider baptism canonically, in the light of the whole of Scripture—Old Testament and New Testament—not from the New Testament alone.

3

PROMISES AND SACRAMENTS

At each stage of covenant history God reinforces his promises by material signs by which he assures us of the truth of what he has said and done. Underlying this is the first sentence in the Bible, Genesis 1:1, 'In the beginning God created the heavens and the earth.' God created both matter and spirit and so uses matter as a vehicle for transmitting spiritual grace. Christianity is not something confined to the 'spiritual' dimension; it involves the whole of life.

The creation, incarnation and bodily resurrection are proof of this. These lie right at the heart of the Christian faith. God brought the universe into existence. The biblical account of creation focuses attention on the material world. We read little or nothing about the creation of the angels. We know God made them but we are not told when or how. The interest of Genesis is entirely in human life in our own particular physical domain. Angels and demons appear; the serpent suddenly comes on the scene in chapter 3, while unfallen angels feature in the account of Abraham (Gen. 18:1–19:22). Yet there is no indication of their origin, other than that the Bible portrays them as creatures. So, while God created all things, including the spiritual realm, it is the physical and visible world that takes centre stage.

The incarnation also directs us in the same path. The eternal Son of God took human nature into personal union, body as well as soul. He lived as man, growing from infancy to childhood to adulthood. He experienced all the range of human experiences, from growth, hunger and thirst to suffering, temptation, bereavement and death. In doing this, the Son of God experienced the world of matter and consequently redeemed it; we are material beings and the entire creation awaits its glorious liberation at Christ's return. Both now and for ever the Son has a human body.

Moreover, central to the gospel is the amazing truth that Christ died for our sins according to the Scriptures, that he was buried, and that on the third day he rose again from the dead according to the Scriptures (1 Cor. 15:3–4). The physical aspect of creation and redemption is underlined by the resurrection from the dead. On the third day Jesus rose from the tomb and he did so *bodily*. This was no mere appearance. It was a coming back to life in the same body in which he had lived before. While it is true—wonderfully so—that his body was transformed, passing through locked doors, ascending to the Father, now glorified beyond our current conceptions, yet it was the same body that bore the marks of the nail prints from the cross. While, as Paul says, he entered a new phase of life according to the Spirit (*kata pneuma*), Jesus expressly denied that it was as a spirit, emphasising this by eating a piece of broiled fish (Luke 24:36–43, John 20:24–9).

Therefore, we believe in the resurrection of the body. At root we are embodied creatures and salvation includes the redemption of the body. Christianity is not some spiritualized religion that abandons the material aspect of humanity. It is earthy and physical as well as spiritual. To oppose the material nature of the gospel is akin to the heresy of gnosticism, which regarded matter as inherently inferior to the spiritual realm. If that were so, we could not be saved. If our salvation consisted merely in continued existence in a purely spiritual state, it would not be *we ourselves* who would be saved. As Anthony Cross points out, much contemporary thought has lapsed into a form of gnosticism 'with its matter-spirit dualism, which is found in the writings of both Zwingli and Barth.'[17] He also identifies biblical scholars such as James Dunn and Gordon Fee as falling into the same

---

Gnostics believed that matter is inherently inferior to the spiritual, but Christianity is physical as well as spiritual. Opposition to the material nature of the gospel is similar to the heresy of Gnosticism.

category, opposing water-baptism and Spirit-baptism.[18]
This is a problem we will address shortly.

SACRAMENTS REINFORCE
GOD'S COVENANTAL PROMISES

From this, we appreciate the fact that God uses material
signs to reinforce his promises. In the garden of Eden,
before the fall, there was the tree of life (Gen 2:9, cf.
Rev. 22:1–2, 19). Genesis 3:22–4 shows that eating of this
tree was associated with everlasting life. This conclusion
is reinforced in Revelation 22:1–2, where the leaves of the
tree of life are for the healing of the nations.

In the Noachic covenant, which re-established the
creation order after the flood, God appointed the rainbow
as a sign that he would never again flood the earth in
the manner he had recently done (Gen. 8:20–22, 9:8–17).
God instituted circumcision in the Abrahamic covenant
(Gen. 17:3–14). As flesh was removed in circumcision,
so God would remove the heart of unbelief and grant
a new heart and a new spirit (Ezk. 36:25–8, Rom. 2:25–9,
4:9–12, Phil. 3:3). In the Mosaic covenant, the Passover
commemorated Yahweh's mighty deliverance of Israel
from bondage in Egypt so as to inherit the promises of
the Abrahamic covenant (Ex. 12:1–13:16), looking forward
to the new exodus to be accomplished in later years. In
the new covenant Jesus appointed baptism in the name
of the trinity (Matt. 28:19–20) to portray cleansing from
sin and union with him in his death and resurrection.
Furthermore, the Supper he introduced was to be the

point at which his people were to be nourished by his body and blood to eternal life (John 6:47–58, 1 Cor. 10:16–17). He appeals not only to our ears, through the words he utters, but also to our eyes, by the sacramental signs.

THE SIGNS AND THE REALITY

Each of these signs accompanied new stages in the outworking of God's covenant purposes. His actions and words in his covenants were reinforced by the signs. The signs were not the reality; they pointed to the reality much like a signpost directs us to a destination other than itself. The reality and the sign differ. However, in each case the sign is appropriate to the reality. There is a definite and visible connection. The tree of life gives everlasting life. The rainbow denotes the triumph of grace over judgment and appears in certain conditions when it rains, the deluge counterbalanced by the sunshine. The Passover indicates Yahweh passing over and sparing his people from wrath, and guiding them to their inheritance. Washing with water in baptism portrays cleansing from the greater filth of sin. Bread and wine in the Lord's Supper demonstrate Christ feeding and nourishing us to eternal life. While sign and reality are distinct their connection is so close as to be inseparable.

To repeat, these signs point to the reality of God's covenant, as signposts direct us to a destination. The sign and the reality are distinct. Yet the sign is appropriate to the reality, since God has appointed it, instituting it in a manner that visibly expresses his exact purpose.

NOT WHAT WE DO, BUT WHAT GOD DOES

It may be tempting to think of the sacraments as rites which we perform, and therefore simply related to human, priestly and churchly actions. From one angle, this is obviously correct. They are undertaken in the covenant community—Israel in the Old Testament, the church in the New Testament—by priests, family heads, or church ministers. However, that is only part of the picture. Indeed, the main part lies elsewhere. Pre-eminently the sacraments as sacraments are signs for God, and indicate what he has done or will do. They go beyond the surface appearance and bring us into direct contact with eternal realities in which the grace of God is powerfully at work.

First, the tree of life in the garden was not expressly forbidden to Adam until after the fall. It is noted in Genesis 2:9 that it was in the midst of the garden but the concentration at that point is on the tree of the knowledge of good and evil, abstinence from which was the test God gave to Adam in the covenant of life. Failing that test, and falling into sin, Adam reaped the penalty of the covenant, which was death. As a consequence, he and his wife were expelled from Eden and the way back was barred to them by cherubim. These cherubim guarded the way to the tree of life, in case Adam were to eat of it and so live for ever (Gen. 3:22–4). There was an evident connection between eating the fruit of the tree of life and living for ever, just as there was between eating the fruit of the tree of the knowledge of good and evil and experiencing sin and death (Gen. 2:16–17, 3:6–7, 11–22). This could hardly be magic, which never occurs in God's dealings with man. A possible explanation is that, should Adam have remained obedient, he would have been granted access to the tree of life and inherited eternal life for himself and all who were in him.

The tree of life appears again in Revelation 22:1–2, where it is seen beside the river that flows from the heavenly city. Its leaves are 'for the healing of the nations.' Again, this tree brings healing and, with it, life and blessing (Rev. 22:14). Eternal salvation consists in eating from it, while those forbidden to do so are under God's curse (Rev. 22:18–19). The climax of Revelation refers to the consummation of the church's salvation, its deliverance from all the forces of evil that threatened it. In this context, the tree of life is again connected with eternal life, not magically but in a signifying and instrumental sense. Participation in the tree of life, when granted by God, brings eternal life. Exclusion from eating of the tree of life means exclusion from everlasting life.

As is clear from Genesis and Revelation—and everything in between—only God gives life. He is the creator. He put the tree in the garden and placed it alongside the heavenly river. He grants man access to it in the heavenly vision and forbids access to man cast out of the garden by his breach of the covenant of life. Only he gives life because he himself is life. Only he has life in himself (John 5:26). He is able to create contingent life because he is life eternally. Hence, the sign of the tree of life ultimately points us to God himself. Participation in the tree is a gift he gives, over which he has sovereign rights.

In the Noachic covenant, God gives another sign. He puts the rainbow in the sky as a sign that he will never again judge the earth by means of a flood. Every time we see the rainbow we can recall this covenant promise, made to the entire human race. The earth will remain so long as God intends it to do so and, meanwhile the regular patterns of day and night, and the seasons of the year, will recur; never again will a universal judgment take place by flood (Gen. 8:20–22, 9:11). However, this sign of the Noachic covenant—note how it is appropriate to the reality of the promise—is a sign first to God before it is a sign to us. God says, 'This is the sign of the covenant that I make between me and you and every living creature that is with you, for all future generations: I have set my bow in the cloud, and it shall be a sign of the covenant between me and the earth. *When I bring clouds over the earth and the bow is seen in the clouds, I will remember my covenant that is between me and you and every living creature of all flesh.* And the waters shall never again become a flood to destroy all flesh. When the bow is in the clouds, *I will see it and remember the everlasting covenant between God and every living creature of all flesh that is on the earth.*' (Gen. 9:12–17). Here the sign is something God himself notes. His own recognition of the sacraments he has appointed impacts his fulfilment of those signs.

In both cases the major point in the sacrament is not what we do but what God does. These are not seen mainly as human actions, as rites which we perform. Over and above this, these are signs for God and demonstrate what he does. The whole force of circumcision, as its significance is unfolded later and in the New Testament, is that only God can change us, declaring us righteous in Christ, and granting us a new heart and a new spirit. The Passover represents the great deliverance accomplished by Yahweh in redeeming Israel from Egypt. The Hebrews were helpless in the face of Pharaoh's persecuting might and cried out to Yahweh for help. If, after escaping Egypt, they had been left to their own devices they would never have reached their eventual inheritance. Not only were the obstacles great, they themselves hankered over what they had left behind and longed to return to Egypt.

And so with baptism and the Lord's Supper, the focus is not so much on the human actions of administering the sacraments but on the mighty acts of God connected with them. Baptism is into the one name of the Father, the Son, and the Holy Spirit. Self-evidently we are dealing here with more than a purely human activity. Baptism is something that belongs to God. The concerted, harmonious and indivisible action of all three persons of the trinity is at stake. Therefore when we consider baptism we must recognize before we start that it is with the living God that we have to do.

GOD KEEPS HIS APPOINTMENTS

God is not arbitrary or capricious. He does not come to us on a whim. He is faithful. When he commits himself to his people he remains committed, now and for ever. He is not some unpredictable despot. The coming of the Spirit at Pentecost was not as some evanescent or transitory 'visitor' but as a permanent resident (John 14:14–23). Not only are the sacraments pre-eminently signs in which God is at work but behind them is the glorious reality that God keeps his appointments.

When Christ died on the cross it was not on any old day, for it was on the day of the Passover, as the authors of the synoptic gospels recount and as Paul recalls (1 Cor. 5:7). Jesus died and rose again at the Passover, 'when the time had fully come' (Gal. 4:4). He was the Passover lamb. The Passover dramatically foreshadowed him and his work. It was at the Passover that he offered himself by the eternal Spirit to the Father (Heb. 9:14). The slaughter of the sacrificial lamb signified the deliverance Yahweh had given to his people from the bondage of Egypt. Now a greater deliverance had arrived, from sin and death, through the Messiah. That deliverance was effected not on any day but on *this* day.

When he rose from the dead it was on the first day of the week. It marked a new epoch, a new creation, just as this had been foreshadowed when the angel announced to Mary the impending birth of Jesus in terms reminiscent of the creation account in Genesis 1:2—'the Holy Spirit will come upon you and the power of the Most High will overshadow you' (Luke 1:34–5). This new creation broke through on the *first* day of the week.

When the Holy Spirit came it was when the day of Pentecost had fully come (Acts 2:1f), not a day earlier, not a day later, precisely on time. It did not happen on the spur of the moment. It was a day fixed by God from eternity, a day that happened to coincide with one of the great festivals he had set up centuries earlier with precisely this in mind. This day was not intended merely as an occasion for ritual, for something humans did. It was selected by God for a decisive staging point in the history of redemption he had planned from before the foundation of the earth.

So, as Paul recounts, 'when the time had fully come God sent forth his Son' (Gal. 4:4). He sent him at just the right time, at the time of his appointment. Or as Luke recalls, 'when the day of Pentecost had fully come,' the Spirit fell on the church (Acts 2:1). In short, God honoured the feast days he had set in the Old Testament. These were not arbitrary or accidental dates on the calendar. God invested them with great significance. From the human side the ritual was no mere empty repetition. It pointed to a reality to be fulfilled expressly in connection with, and through, the ritual. God brought that fulfilment precisely in and through those days he had established. We shall see how this relates to Christian baptism in the following chapters.

God honoured the feasts he established in the Old Testament. They were given for a purpose. That purpose was fulfilled in these great climactic events. When God promises, and seals these promises in the signs he appoints, he is not deceiving us. He honours his appointments, he comes as he promised, the reality to which the signs point is brought about in connection with them. These Old Testament feast days and covenantal signs all pointed to God's great acts of salvation to be realised in his Son, Jesus Christ.

 Baptism is first and foremost a divine activity. God is at work and he honours his promises given in connection with it.

4

THE INDIVIDUAL

AND THE CORPORATE

In our culture we think of everyone as an individual; Bill Smith, Mary Jones, and so on. When we count the size of a congregation we enumerate it in terms of individual people, such as two hundred and twenty three. The United Kingdom tax system now treats each person as a separate entity for tax purposes; husbands and wives are not relevant categories.

AN INSEPARABLE CONNECTION

Our situation is very different from the context of the biblical authors. In both Old Testament and New

Testament, people were considered to be relational beings. Their individuality was placed in the context of the family, the tribe, or the nation. Thus we read of David *the son of Jesse, of the tribe of Judah*. It indicates that we do not live in a vacuum but have an inheritance from the past. This is based on the created nature of man. Humans were not made to be isolated individuals but relational. God created man as male and female, together in relation the one to the other, and to God in whose image they were (Gen. 1:26ff). A typical example of this, one amongst a profusion of similar instances, occurs in 2 Chronicles 20:14: 'And the Spirit of the Lord came upon Jahaziel the son of Zechariah, son of Benaiah, son of Jeiel, son of Mattaniah, a Levite of the sons of Asaph, in the midst of the assembly.' Jahaziel, as any other person in the Old Testament, was seen as related to his ancestors. You were A the son of B the son of C; your historical antecedents identified you as who you were. Moreover, you were also related to your tribe; in Jahaziel's case, the tribe of Levi—there was a contemporary, geographical relatedness. In this, humans reflect in a creaturely manner the relationality of God, who is not a monad but a trinity. Hence, the Spirit of the Lord came upon Jahaziel in the midst of the assembly—in the corporate, relational context, not in private isolation.

This comes to expression very starkly in Joshua 7. Israel's triumphant march through Canaan was abruptly halted at Ai by a savage and tragic defeat. Eventually the cause was traced to unfaithfulness on the part of a man named Achan (vv. 16–18). Achan's sin occasioned Israel's defeat and incidentally brought about an unwanted loss of life (v. 5). The point is that when Achan sinned 'all Israel sinned' (v.11). The individual and the corporate were inseparably connected. One of the closest examples today is a sports team. If, with the score 2–2 and only seconds left, the goalkeeper lets a soft shot trickle into the net, the whole team loses because of his mistake. That this is not confined to the Old Testament is clear when Paul says to the Corinthian church 'if one member suffers, all suffer together; if one member is honoured, all rejoice together' (1 Cor. 12:26).

INDIVIDUAL RESPONSIBILITY

This biblical stress on the corporate does not blur personal accountability. The Mosaic legislation intended for Israel's life in the land of Canaan stipulated that each person was responsible for his own sin (Deut. 24:16). Later, when some were using their corporate solidarity with their ancestors in an attempt to evade responsibility for their own wrong doing, the prophet rebuked them severely. Whereas these renegades were saying 'the fathers have eaten sour grapes and the children's teeth are set on edge' (Ezek. 18:1–2), Ezekiel insisted that 'the soul that sins shall die' (Ezek. 18:4). From a more upbeat perspective, this principle points to the fact that the individual lives and flourishes in the context of the community. That is how God made us—in his own image, male and female, related to one another and to God, who himself speaks as plural and relational (Gen. 1:26–27).

SALVATION IN THE NEW TESTAMENT

Paul describes our salvation in this same way. When Adam fell into sin and death, the whole race fell in him. Salvation is found in union with the second Adam, Jesus Christ, whose obedience has more than remedied Adam's failure (Rom. 5:12–21). Adam brought death, Christ brings life (1 Cor. 15:20–58). In Adam—in Christ; the whole saga of sin and salvation hinges on these realities.[19] This is not how the gospel has been presented in modern evangelicalism; it is evangelicalism which has drifted from the truth.[20] This is not the free-wheeling individualism of the modern western world, or of the American frontier. Nor is it the drab suppression of the individual seen in Marxist or Islamic countries. The one and the many, the individual and the community flourish together.

The identical principle holds true on a lower level. On the day of Pentecost, Peter declared that salvation is offered to the hearers *and their children* (Acts 2:39). Not only those present to hear his message but their children also were the proper recipients of Peter's call to repentance. In the background is the declaration by Moses, shortly before his death, that the covenant Yahweh made with Israel at Sinai forty years before was actually made with the children of that generation, those who were alive at this later time (Deut. 5:1–5).

Two passages in particular strikingly reinforce this principle, passages that have largely escaped the radar of individualistically rooted readers, preachers and scholars. In the synoptic gospels, there is an account of Jesus healing a paralysed man who was lowered through an open roof by his friends, since the entrance to the building where Jesus was preaching was blocked by a large crowd (Mark 2:1–12, Matt. 9:1–8, Luke 5:18–26). In each account we read that Jesus, *seeing their faith*, said to the paralytic, your sins are forgiven. The paralysed man was healed, and his sins forgiven, in connection with the faith of those who brought him. Again, in the famous passage in the Letter of James, where prayer is prescribed for the sick, the sick person is to call for the elders 'and let them pray over him...and the prayer of faith will save the one who is sick, and the Lord will raise him up' (Jas. 5:13–18). *The elders' prayer of faith for the sick person* will be the occasion of the invalid's healing and forgiveness. In neither of these cases should we think that the paralytic or the sick person lacked faith of their own. Presumably their actions embodied faith and they were also included in the plural subject. Indeed, the sick man is seen as calling for the elders for this very reason. However, the point to note is that *the faith of the group is cited as the significant piece of information*, not the faith of a particular individual.

On Paul's missionary journeys, the jailor at Philippi is brought to faith in Christ in a sudden and remarkable way (Acts 16:25–34), whereupon he and his family are baptized (vv. 32–3). After this 'he rejoiced along with his entire household, *he having believed in God*' (v. 34). The entire household are baptized and rejoice, since he has believed in God! Again, we do not have evidence to conclude that the rest of the household did *not* themselves believe. However, the members of the household—all of them, the entire household—rejoice because of the faith of their head. The corporate unit is again highlighted as the significant item.

This is so even when a person is apparently unmarried. Lydia, identified as a prosperous business woman, whose work took her from Thyatira across the Aegean to Philippi, nevertheless was the head of her own house and ministered to the apostles accordingly (Acts 16:14–15). In such cases, the single person is seen as having his or her own household.

This principle is seen by Luke as decisive for the entire future ministry of the Christian church. The setting was the first church council at which Peter was interrogated over his preaching to the Gentiles and eating with them, the latter practice being forbidden to Jews. Indeed, Peter was only persuaded to accept the Roman centurion Cornelius' summons to come to his house after a special vision repeated twice (Acts 10:9–23). It was a radical new step, a decisive point in the history of the church, since it signalled the start of the Gentile mission that continues to this day. In recounting what happened, Peter announces that the angel had declared to Cornelius that the gospel was directed to him *and all his household* (Acts 11:14). This council set the foundation stone for the ministry of the church ever after. Its decision was that the message of salvation is for individuals *and the household to which they belong*, not to individuals in isolation. This is in continuity with Joshua's call for faithfulness to God's covenant and his declaration that he *and his house* would follow the Lord (Josh. 24:15). It is worth repeating—what a stark contrast this is to modern Western society, where each person is reckoned as a discrete individual in isolation from any particular group or larger social entity!

THE FOUNDATION—THE NATURE OF GOD

The church has confessed down through the centuries that the Father, the Son, and the Holy Spirit are three eternally distinct persons, in indivisible union. Simultaneously the three are indivisibly one. The one being of God and the three persons are equally ultimate. If the one was absolute and the persons derivative, the result would be the modalist heresy; God's revelation as the Father, the Son, and the Holy Spirit would not reflect who he eternally is in himself. If that were the case, we could not be saved since we would not have received a true revelation of God, since the Son who came to save us would not be God-in-himself. On the other hand, if the three were ultimate and the one being of God derivative, we would have tritheism. Alternatively, if the Son and the Holy Spirit were lesser beings than the Father, we could not worship the Son, for he would

The modalist heresy treats the one being of God as absolute and the three persons as derivative so that the Father, the Son, and the Holy Spirit do not reflect who God is in himself. The church's confession of God as three eternally distinct persons in indivisible union is the biblical foundation for a proper understanding of the individual and the corporate in Scripture.

be less than God, and consequently could not have saved us. Each of these alternatives are heretical since, if true, they would falsify the Christian faith.

No, God is eternally one being who is the Father, the Son, and the Holy Spirit. Each person is entirely God and all that can be said to be God is in each. As Gerald Bray put it, they occupy the same infinite divine space.[21] This is the new covenant name of God—the one name of the Father, the Son, and the Holy Spirit—named over each and every one of the members of the new covenant (Matt. 28:18–20).[22]

God has stamped vestiges of his unity-in-diversity throughout creation. The heavens declare the glory of God (Ps. 19:1–6). The invisible things of God have been clearly seen in creation since it was made (Rom. 1:18–20). The philosophical problem of the one and the many has been debated through history. God created humans in his own image, male and female. Humanity is relational. Each particular human being is a distinct individual but finds his or her identity in relation to others and to God.

The Bible preserves this balance between individual responsibility existing in a corporate context. God has established three main institutions for the maintenance and development of human life; the family, the state, and the church. All have their own proper sphere, according to the wise provision of God, which human societies abandon to their own detriment. The family is the context in which people are born, raised and nurtured. The state exists to protect life, administer justice, and provide the means for families to flourish. The church

exists to worship God and to spread the gospel of Christ
to the ends of the earth. It means that the household
retains an integral place in the purposes of God.

TAKE A CORPORATE VIEW

Therefore when we consider our salvation, the covenant
by which it is brought to us, and the sacraments that
attend it, we should see it in this corporate manner. We
are all saved in the context of the church. In whatever
way people arrive at saving faith in Jesus Christ it is
in connection with the ministry of the church. Even
if it is through reading a page of the Bible washed up
in a bottle on a desert island, it is through the writings
of the apostles and prophets that faith comes, the same
apostles and prophets who are the foundation of the
church. As Cyprian put it, 'he cannot have God for his
Father who does not have the church for his mother.'[23]
Augustine added that 'outside the church sins are not
remitted. For the church has the pledge of the Holy
Spirit, without which there is no remission of sins.'[24]

Calvin echoed Augustine in his comment that, 'away
from her [the church's] bosom one cannot hope for any
forgiveness of sins or any salvation.'[25] In the church we
flourish, our gifts are used to the common good. It is in
the company of the whole church of the redeemed that
we will enter heaven.

As in Israel in the Old Testament, where the family,
tribe and nation was integral to God's redemptive
purpose, and the individual found his or her place in terms

of relationships of kinship, so in the New Testament the individual is part of the church, which in turn continues to be based upon households and families.

 We should see baptism, as part of our place in God's saving purposes, in a corporate context.

PART TWO

WHAT BAPTISM SIGNIFIES

In this second section we will ask about the meaning of baptism as the New Testament presents it to us. Often baptism is considered either to be a symbol or a picture of God's grace in Jesus Christ or else of our own obedience. However, have we missed something here? Bearing in mind the questions we explored in Part One, how far have we thought of baptism in relation to the Old Testament, or considered how it applies not only to us as individuals but to our families? How far have we understood it in connection with the gospel of Christ or with the whole sweep of the plan of God for the renovation of the universe? Have we viewed it simply as a rite, an action that we do because Christ commanded it, but signifying or conveying nothing in itself? We need at least to be open to the possibility that the teaching of the apostles may have been missed due to layers of tradition developed in the modern world.

In these three chapters we will explore the connection between baptism and cleansing from sin, as described in the New Testament. In tandem with that, we will consider how far the apostles connect baptism to our receiving the Holy Spirit. Both these themes surface on the Day of Pentecost, when Peter calls his hearers to repent and be baptized, for the remission of sins and the gift of the Holy Spirit (Acts 2:38–9). What exactly is the connection between the sacrament of baptism and the reality to which it points?

Chapter 6 will consider Paul's teaching about baptism and union with Christ in his death and resurrection. This is prominent in Romans 6 but it also appears elsewhere. It is here that it is frequently argued that baptism and regeneration are related, since regeneration is akin to a resurrection. How are we to do justice to these passages? Is baptism purely symbolic or is God's grace connected with it? If the latter is true, in what way are we to view such a connection? What was the teaching of the Reformers or the classic Reformed confessions on this matter?

Chapter 7 will then get to grips with the sometimes vexed question of who should be baptized. It is obvious from the New Testament that baptism and faith go together. It is equally clear that adult converts should be baptized on profession of faith. However, how do the children of believers fit this picture? Here our earlier discussion about the connection between the Old Testament and the New Testament is important. We will explore the relationship of the New covenant to the Abrahamic covenant, the individual to the household in the New Testament, and particularly the relative priority of God's grace to our own faith.

This section is the theological heart of the matter. In order to ponder it well, we need to have considered carefully the basic principles explained in the first section, for these underlie—in one way or another—our thought on the central issues of this part.

5

CLEANSING FROM SIN

In baptism, water is used. Everyone knows that. John the Baptist carried out his baptisms in the River Jordan or at Aenon 'as there was a lot of water there' (Jn. 3:23). When Philip was travelling in the chariot with the Ethiopian eunuch they stopped at an oasis for Philip to baptize the man since there was water present (Acts 8:36). Later, Peter recognized that Cornelius and his guests, on whom the Spirit had fallen, should not be forbidden to receive baptism by water (Acts 10:46–47). Questions have arisen over precisely how much water is needed. The Greek verb *baptidzo* has the main meaning of 'to dip', but it can also mean 'to sprinkle'. However, there is another verb, *hrantidzo*, that means 'to sprinkle,' so the choice of *baptidzo* may—at least on some occasions—possibly intentionally denote dipping or immersion.

The Greek Church, which knows a thing or two about its own language, has always practised immersion.[26] As for Rome, the *Catechism of the Catholic Church* states that 'baptism is performed in the most expressive way by triple immersion in the baptismal water. However, from ancient times it has also been able to be conferred by pouring the water three times over the candidate's head.'[27] The 1552 *Boke of Common Prayer and Administracion of the Sacramentes, and Other Rites and Ceremonies in the Churche of England* specified that 'the Priest shal take the childe in his handes, and…shal dippe it in the water, so it be discretely and warely done.' However, 'yf the child be weke, it shall suffyce to power water upon it.'[28] After an extensive debate, the Westminster Assembly agreed by a narrow margin on the lawfulness of dipping, while holding that sprinkling or pouring was the most appropriate mode.[29] Credobaptists do not have proprietorial rights over immersion; the practice is much older than their churches. Indeed, in the early stages of the Reformation, the Reformers were inclined to favour immersion.[30]

However, apart from the Orthodox and many credo-baptists, there is general agreement that the mode of baptism is not the most important thing and that it can be administered by sprinkling, pouring or immersion. In terms of its visual and symbolic character, each of these portrays a particular aspect of baptism.

WHEN SHOULD SOMEONE BE BAPTISED?

Since baptism is mentioned first in Jesus' programme for the discipling of the nations (Matt. 28:18–20) it is paradigmatic for the church and its mission: 'Make all nations disciples, baptizing them in the [one] name of the Father, and the Son, and the Holy Spirit; teaching them to obey everything I have commanded you.' Baptism is the sacrament of initiation in the new covenant, administered in the new covenant name of the blessed and most holy trinity.[31] From this, the church has acknowledged that baptism in the name of the trinity is valid from whatever source, since the sacrament does not belong to any particular church but to the triune God.

It is obvious, from the record in Acts, that the apostles did not delay in baptizing. Even at the risk that a person might fall away from the faith afterwards, they baptized immediately a person could be called a Christian. The tragic possibility of apostasy always exists and it cannot be made the basis for a delay in baptism, since even the most meticulous teaching is not of itself sufficient to prevent it. This proved true when Simon showed himself to be motivated by power and greed (Acts 8:9–24). That there can be no guarantee that any one person baptized will not fall away at some point is evident from the many heretics and false teachers that sprang up during New Testament times and the implication that some of the community to which The Letter to the Hebrews was addressed had publicly repudiated Christ (Heb. 6:1–8, 10:26–31).

BAPTISM AS CLEANSING FROM SIN

Baptism is a form of washing. Water has the property of cleansing. Since the sacraments as signs are appropriately related to the reality they signify, it is not surprising that baptism is described as the washing away of sin. Paul was told by Ananias to 'rise and be baptized, and wash away your sins, calling on his name' (Acts 22:16). Here there is a clear allusion to baptism being in the name of the Father, the Son, and the Holy Spirit. Calling upon the name of the Lord is a phrase often used for an act of worship.

Paul refers in his letters to baptism as washing. Christ loves the church and cleanses it by the washing of water with the Word (Eph. 5:26). Here the ministry of the Word and the sacrament are means by which the church is purified and cleansed. Writing to Titus about the grace of God which brought the Gentiles out of slavery to sin, Paul attributes this to the kindness and love of our God and Saviour, according to his mercy. In this 'he saved us through the washing of regeneration and renewal of the Holy Spirit' (Tit. 3:5). This statement has usually been understood by the church through the ages as referring to the Spirit working in and through our baptism.[32] Baptism is the washing common to all the church and would readily have been understood to be in view. At one of the leading Protestant synods, the Westminster Assembly, Titus 3:5 was one of the most frequently cited texts in its extensive debates on the theology and practice of baptism. Furthermore, Paul addresses those who became Christian from a dissolute background, laden with a range of major sins. He says to them; 'but you were washed, you were sanctified, you were justified, in the name of the Lord Jesus and in the Spirit of our God' (1 Cor. 6:11). Paul was accustomed to use the word *theos* (God) for the Father. From this it follows that he refers to a washing in the name of the trinity, all three persons indivisibly active. You were washed in the name of the Lord Jesus and in the Spirit of our Father—the baptismal reference is clear-cut. This cleansing washing he connects with their being transferred from the kingdom of darkness to the body of Christ—sanctification in its primary, spatial meaning— and their being declared righteous in union with Christ. We have echoes of this in Jesus' comments to Nicodemus, in stressing the necessity for him to be born 'of water and the Spirit' in order to enter the kingdom of God (John 3:5). Baptism is the entry point, the place at which a decisive transfer occurs from sin to faith, from being in Adam to being in Christ, for it is the moment when discipleship begins, in accordance with Jesus' last words to his apostles.

BAPTISM AND THE RECEPTION OF THE SPIRIT

Since there is a definite connection between baptism and cleansing from sin it follows that there is some kind of relationship too between baptism and our reception of the Holy Spirit. This follows from the Spirit being the one who grants us faith and repentance, and by whose work we are cleansed from sin through the atoning death of Christ.

Indeed, this connection is explicit in the New Testament. On the Day of Pentecost, Peter announced to his hearers that they must repent and be baptized 'for the remission of sins and you will receive the gift of the Holy Spirit' (Acts 2:37–9); repentance and baptism on the one hand, forgiveness of sins and the Holy Spirit on the other. In Scripture, faith is inseparable from repentance. Some might balk at the inclusion of baptism here. However, we recall that the material and spiritual are distinct realms but nevertheless inseparable, and that God conveys his grace through material means. Evidently baptism in Peter's mind is more than a mere symbol of something detached from it. There is a certain instrumentality to it. At the same time, since Peter mentions the Holy Spirit he points beyond human action to divine grace. Our faith and repentance cannot secure or earn our salvation, or gain us the gift of the Holy Spirit, and neither can baptism. These are the means through which the grace of God operates, much like Naaman dipping in the despised River Jordan for cleansing from leprosy (2 Kings 5:1–14). Behind this is the baptism of Jesus, which foreshadowed his greater baptism on the cross (Matt. 3:13–15, cf. Luke 12:49–50). Immediately afterwards, as Jesus was coming out of the water, heaven was 'torn open,' the Holy Spirit descended and rested on him in the form of a dove, and the voice of the Father publicly declared him to be his beloved Son. The connection between baptism and the Spirit could hardly be clearer.

It is striking that no consistent pattern emerges between baptism and the reception of the Spirit. In Acts 2, Peter implies that the gift of the Spirit will follow repentance and baptism. In Paul's case, his filling with the Spirit and his baptism take place at the same time, the former possibly through Ananias' laying on of hands (Acts 9:17–18). With Cornelius and his guests, the Spirit descends on them while they listen to Peter's message, whereupon Peter commands them to be baptized (Acts 10:34–48). While there is no fixed temporal order yet, as Paul wrote to the Corinthians, the Spirit baptized *us all* into the one body of Christ; the Spirit, baptism and union with Christ are each part of a complex of connections, whether viewed in redemptive-historical terms as a once-for-all happening, or in its ongoing outworking (1 Cor. 12:13).

BAPTISM, UNION WITH CHRIST AND SALVATION

1 Peter 3:21 states that 'baptism saves you.' This statement has been used to justify the idea that the sacraments work grace by the fact of their being performed (the Roman Catholic doctrine) so that baptism is necessary for salvation. It has also been evaded as uncomfortable or explained as pure symbolism. Neither are satisfactory alternatives. What does the context tell us about Peter's intention?

Peter was writing to churches enduring persecution (vv. 14–17). He compares their situation with Noah's isolation while building the ark, implicitly condemning his contemporaries and no doubt receiving ridicule and abuse for doing so (v. 20). Above all, Peter points his readers to Christ, who suffered 'the righteous for the unrighteous' (v. 18). In both cases, Noah and Christ were vindicated—Noah by the ark, in which he was rescued from the flood, Christ in his resurrection. In verses 19–21 Peter makes a parenthetical digression. His chain of thought, broken off at the end of verse 18, is not resumed until verse 22; it runs '[Christ] put to death in the flesh, made alive by the Spirit [in his resurrection]...who has gone into heaven and is at the right hand of God.' This was Christ's triumphant vindication by the Father; it is intended to buttress the faith of the struggling churches. The digression in verses 19–21—one of the most difficult passages in the Bible—refers to Christ's actions in his resurrection when he was 'made alive by the Spirit'; he proclaimed condemnation to the fallen angels, particularly those that worked behind the scenes in Noah's time. Noah was saved through the ark, he says, whereas you are saved through baptism. In both instances God graciously saves, but he saves through means. In the case of baptism Peter makes clear 'baptism now saves you...through the resurrection of Jesus Christ.'[33]

In short, God's salvation for his church is achieved by Jesus Christ in his resurrection. Peter's view of union with Christ is remarkably close to Paul's. He has already stated that we have been 'born again to a living hope through the resurrection of Jesus Christ' (1 Pet. 1:3). Christ was raised from the dead; we share in that resurrection, as a rebirth. We do so since we are united to him. He was brought into new, transcendent life and in union with him so were we. Consequently, in chapter 3, Peter affirms that we share in the vindication of Christ, in his resurrection. Christ's death and resurrection is his baptism[34] and it is that which saves us by virtue of our union with him, our being incorporated into Christ. To that great reality baptism itself is inseparably fused. The connection with water is obvious in verses 19–21; the ark saved Noah and he was vindicated in the waters, as the persecuted churches to which Peter wrote are saved by the resurrection of Christ in and through baptism. We recall the relationship between the tree of life and eternal life in Genesis and Revelation. In both cases, the sign and reality are distinct but inseparable, the sign appropriate to the reality to which it points and with which it is connected.

IS BAPTISM PURELY SYMBOLIC?

What is the precise connection between the sacrament and the reality, between the baptism and the cleansing? Is it purely symbolic? We have seen enough, I suggest, to reject that idea. Certainly the sacraments are full of symbolism. Yet there is an efficacy attached to them that goes far beyond a mere visual aid. Besides, an exclusively symbolic interpretation tends to rest on a dualistic view of the relationship of spirit to matter that is foreign to the Bible.

Is the grace signified in baptism, the reality itself, to be regarded as *parallel* to its outward manifestation? Does it mean that as we are washed with the baptismal waters, so also—in parallel as it were—the Holy Spirit grants us grace, faith, repentance, and above all himself? This has been called 'symbolic parallelism.' Or is what is signified actually *effected* by the Spirit? Does the Spirit bring this to pass by baptism? This is sometimes called 'symbolic instrumentalism.'[35]

The Roman Catholic Church holds that baptism, as the other sacraments, is effective by the fact of its being performed. When a baby is born it must be baptized at once in case it were suddenly to die. This rests upon its belief that baptism is necessary for salvation. Hence, Rome makes provision, in an emergency, for baptism by midwives or laypersons. Lutheranism also has a highly objective view of baptism. It conveys grace efficaciously unless it is resisted. With both the vital role of faith in the recipient appears to be downplayed.

Most modern evangelicalism operates at the other extreme. It has a purely symbolic view of baptism. It is a visual aid. Immersion portrays union with Christ in his death and resurrection. We see the one baptized plunged under water and rising again. Others, who practice baptism by sprinkling, see it as portraying cleansing from sin. Of course, union with Christ and cleansing from sin are not mutually exclusive. Many view baptism as an

'In the New Testament salvation, union with Christ, forgiveness, washing, regeneration and receiving the Holy Spirit are all attributed to baptism.' 'This may not accord with the view of the majority of Evangelicals today but they should take up their complaint with the apostles' (Tony Lane).[36]

act of human obedience, a testimony to grace already received. However, in each of these common evangelical positions, the connection between baptismal sign and the reality is largely incidental.

Probably to most evangelicals today, who view material actions and the conveyance of spiritual grace as separate, the description of baptism in the New Testament is alien. For them, 1 Peter 3:21 and similar statements are at best puzzling. This is at odds with the strong view of the connection between baptism and salvation in the New Testament, and with the theology of union with Christ that underlies it. We must ask whether the truth lies somewhere between the extremes of Rome and today's non-sacramentalism.

How is this strong language about baptism compatible with justification only by faith, and salvation by grace? This will occupy our attention in the next two chapters.

6

UNION WITH CHRIST

Baptism is a sign and a seal of the grace of God in Jesus Christ as it to expression in his covenant. Baptism admits the person baptized into the visible church. This is clear from the nature of baptism, as the first thing to be done in the discipling of the nations (Matt. 28:19–20), and from the regular pattern in the Book of Acts. However, baptism is more than an admission into the visible church. It is also a sign and seal of the covenant of grace. It is a sign because it is a sacrament, and so points to something it signifies. It seals it because it is a mark of ownership, for Christ has taken the one baptized as his own. The covenant of grace, of which baptism is a sign and seal, consists of engrafting into Christ. The one baptized is a member of Christ and thus of his body, the church. Therefore baptism both signifies and seals the covenant blessings of regeneration, remission of sins, and belonging to God through Jesus Christ to live in newness of life (sanctification). A classic Protestant statement brings baptism directly into connection with the whole of salvation, as 'a sign and seal of the covenant of grace, of his [the one baptized's] engrafting into Christ, of regeneration, of remission of sins, and of his giving up unto God, through Jesus Christ, to walk in newness of life.' It signifies these things and it seals them.[37] It is more than admission to the visible church. It is certainly more than a symbolic representation.

A SIGN AND SEAL

Baptism is a sign of engrafting into Christ, and thus of regeneration, renewal, and resurrection. As a sign, baptism points to something other than itself. A signpost directs attention to a place at a certain distance. The signpost's indication of the direction in which a town or village is located will direct one to that place; it is appropriate to the reality to which it points. So also baptism, while it is not to be identified with the reality it signifies and seals, is nevertheless appropriate to it, and related to it. We remarked earlier on how sacraments function at every stage of covenant history, from the Garden of Eden onwards. In each case, there is this connection with the reality promised in the covenant.

A seal is a mark of ownership, and was so understood

UNION WITH CHRIST | 57

in the biblical world as well as in the seventeenth century, when the Westminster Assembly met and the London Baptist Confession was drawn up. In this case, as a seal, baptism marks the one baptized as owned by the holy trinity, in whose name the sacrament is administered. This corresponds with the role of circumcision in the Abrahamic covenant—a seal of the righteousness Abraham had through faith (Rom. 4:11).

GRACE EXHIBITED

Augustine described the sacraments as 'a kind of visible word of God.'[38] Baptism is a sign, graphically portraying union with Christ, by immersion in water, demonstrating our union with Christ in death, burial and resurrection (Rom. 6:1ff), and by sprinkling, pointing to cleansing from sin (Acts 22:16).[39] In this way, the grace of God is made visibly evident. Paul says what is of first importance is that 'Christ died for our sins according to the Scriptures, and that he was buried, and that he rose from the dead on the third day according to the Scriptures' (1 Cor. 15:3–4). This primary point in the gospel is dramatically exhibited in baptism into Christ. The Westminster divines, in using the verb 'exhibit' were stressing something stronger than the word means in our own day. In the seventeenth century, 'exhibit' was closer to 'confer', and contained the idea that what was shown forth was actually given and bestowed to the one to whom it was exhibited.[40]

GRACE CONFERRED

Earlier, we discussed the point that the sacraments are first of all signs for God. In the sacraments God works to confirm his promises and to grant grace. We noted too how he keeps his appointments, having honoured the feasts he established in the Old Testament by his Son dying at Passover and the Spirit being sent at Pentecost. These were not simply dates on the calendar; they were occasions he had planned to fulfil his purposes.

That this pattern is evident with baptism is supported by the strong language the New Testament uses of it. Peter's evangelistic sermon on the Day of Pentecost called on his hearers to repent and be baptized. In return, their sins would be forgiven and they would receive the gift of the Holy Spirit, as the apostles had done: 'Repent and be baptized in the name of Jesus Christ, each one of you, for the remission of your sins, and you will receive the gift of the Holy Spirit' (Acts 2:38–9). Later, Paul was exhorted by Ananias to 'rise and be baptized and wash away your sins' (Acts 22:16). In turn, Peter considers that 'baptism saves you...through the resurrection of Jesus Christ' (1 Pet. 3:21). Just as with the tree of life, the rainbow, circumcision, and the Passover, baptism signifies, seals and exhibits the grace of God, while the Holy Spirit powerfully confers that grace of union with Christ.

This does not mean that God's grace in Christ is given automatically, simply by virtue of being baptized. In contrast to Rome, which views baptism—as the other sacraments—as effective by the fact of its being performed (*ex opere operato*), this grace is received through faith. For Rome, when a baby is born it is imperative for it to be baptized at the earliest opportunity, in case it were to die beforehand. 'From the moment that a sacrament is celebrated in accordance with the intention of the Church, the power of Christ and his Spirit acts in and through it,' according to the *Catechism of the Catholic Church*. Therefore 'in case of necessity, any person, even someone not baptized, can baptize, if he has the required intention.' This arises since 'baptism is necessary for salvation.' In the case of infants who die unbaptized 'the Church can only entrust them to the mercy of God' for we can only hope. 'All the more urgent is the Church's call not to prevent little children coming to Christ through the gift of holy Baptism.'[41]

In contrast, the Reformed hold that the Holy Spirit is sovereign and is not tied to the act of baptism. We are not made a member of Christ, nor regenerated, *because* we have been baptized. From this it follows that grace is not given to a baptized person on the grounds of his baptism. Rather, it is due to the electing grace of God in Christ. That grace is given in baptism 'to those to whom it belongs.'[42] Not all who are baptized will be saved. Saving faith is necessary. That is why, at Pentecost, Peter, alongside his requirement of baptism, coupled the need to repent.

Notwithstanding this caveat, the grace of union with Christ, signified, sealed and exhibited in baptism is conferred by the Holy Spirit. The sacrament has no power of itself to engraft a person into Christ, to regenerate him or bring him to salvation. That this happens is due to the gracious work of the Holy Spirit alone. However, it does not occur independently of baptism but rather in and through it. Once again, baptism—as a sacrament—first and foremost points to what God does. He keeps his appointments, working through the means he has chosen for his purposes. The sign and the reality are fully appropriate and compatible.

God's covenant contains promised blessings but also warnings to those who do not believe or live in disobedience. Baptism, as a sacrament of the new covenant, also conveys a curse as well as blessing. This is clear in 1 Corinthians 10:1ff. However, while unbelief and its consequences occur they are not germane to the purpose of the sacrament but are incidental to it.

This grace of regeneration and union with Christ is received through faith. At a time known only to God, he regenerates a person. This, the New Testament asserts, is connected to the preaching of the Word (Jas. 1:18, 1 Pet. 1:23, Rom. 10:14–17); it is not tied to the Word but neither is it separated from it. It happens *with* the Word preached. However, regeneration is also connected to baptism. Regeneration may be at the instant of the baptism. It could be many years afterwards or it may happen earlier, even from the mother's womb, as in the case of John the Baptist. When an adult convert is baptized one is to assume that regeneration has already occurred, since he or she will be baptized on profession of faith. Yet a connection between baptism and regeneration there is. It is not automatic, it is not temporal, it is not logical; *it is theological.*

In order to understand this, we need to remember that both baptism and regeneration take place at the very point at which a person can be regarded as a Christian. The regenerating activity of the Holy Spirit is the occasion that enables a person to believe savingly in Christ; without it we would all remain trapped in our sin and unbelief. It is the precise moment when our Christian life begins. So too, baptism was administered in the New Testament immediately an adult professed faith. There was no delay. Baptism is to be the first step in the process of discipling the nations (Matt. 28:18–20). The apostles were prepared to risk baptizing people who later turned away from the faith—Simon is a prime example (Acts 8:9–24)—such was the directness of the connection.

Moreover, regeneration is a resurrection, as Peter puts it in 1 Peter 1:3. We have been 'born [or begotten] again…through the resurrection of Jesus Christ from the dead.' We are united to Christ in his resurrection as we are in his death and burial. This union takes effect as we share in Christ's resurrection in our regeneration and all that follows. Paul, in similar fashion, refers to our being united with Christ in his resurrection, and thus renewed to newness of life (Rom. 6:1ff). In Ephesians the resurrection motif is again present, when Paul considers we have been made alive together with Christ. The allied concept of a new creation comes into the picture in

2 Corinthians 5:17. This epochal moment is marked by baptism. Baptism is into union with Christ in his death and resurrection and, since we are regenerated in union with Christ's resurrection, our baptism and regeneration are inseparably connected in a theological sense.

DIVERGENT INTERPRETATIONS

Following Karl Barth, some New Testament scholars such as James Dunn and Gordon Fee, have made a sharp separation between what they call 'Spirit-baptism' and 'water-baptism.'[43] By this distinction, passages that have historically been understood to refer to baptism are seen instead to describe the work of the Spirit in regeneration, or to the Spirit baptizing the corporate body of Christ. This line of thought is mistaken for a number of reasons. First, and by no means to be discounted, it departs from the uniform belief of expositors throughout the history of the Christian church. It may possibly be that fifty generations of theologians and believers were all wrong; however, to establish that overwhelming evidence is needed. Second, this theory implies a major nature-grace dualism, a radical separation of the material and the spiritual, with far-reaching ontological implications. It creates a novel dichotomy where none was ever understood to exist before. It drives a wedge between the material and the spiritual, in a way more akin to gnosticism than the Christian faith. We have argued that throughout Scripture God's spiritual grace operates through material means; the two are distinct but inseparable. We saw that much Greek thought regarded the material was decidedly inferior to the spiritual; gnosticism took this even further. Thirdly, it also posits an erroneous dichotomy between the individual and the corporate, whereas as we have argued the two stand together throughout the Bible. In each of these ways, this claim stems from analytic thinking, by which constituent elements are considered separately and in isolation, rather than from synthetic thought which sees the connections and thinks them together.

Two notable attempts have been made recently to dispute the point that Paul is talking about baptism in Romans 6, where he insists that Christians do not live in sin because they are united to Christ in his death and resurrection.

> Are we to continue in sin that grace may abound? By no means! How can we who died to sin still live in it? Do you not know that all of us who have been baptized into Christ Jesus were baptized into his death? We were buried therefore with him by baptism into death, in order that, just as Christ was raised from the dead by the glory of the Father, we too might walk in newness of life (Rom. 6:1–4).[44]

D.M. Lloyd-Jones, in his edited lectures on Romans, dismissed any connection with baptism here on the grounds that such a view was 'sacramentarian' and asserted that the grace of God was transmitted in the water, that it is 'the act of baptizing that, in and of itself, unites the person baptized with the Lord Jesus Christ.' This is a fairly—but not entirely—accurate description of Roman Catholic sacramentalism but Lloyd-Jones happily lumped it with positions such as the 'Anglican, Scottish and many others.'[45] His argument is that Paul is concerned in Romans 6 with union with Christ, not baptism. Preoccupation with baptism detracts from union with Christ. Paul's reference to baptism, Lloyd-Jones argued, is to baptism by the Holy Spirit into Christ: 'baptism by water is not in the mind of the Apostle at all in these two verses; instead it is the baptism that is wrought by the Spirit.'[46]

To my mind, Lloyd-Jones makes the two cardinal errors we discussed above. He operates from a dualistic perspective where material things cannot be the vehicle of spiritual grace. As a consequence, water-baptism is separated from Spirit-baptism, the Holy Spirit baptizing us into the body of Christ. This form of dualism has implications much wider than to baptism alone. The second problem is that such a disjunction rests on an analytic form of thought whereby realities are distinguished from each other and separated in atomistic fashion, rather than seen in their integral interconnections. 'Distinct but inseparable' is a pattern that recurs throughout theology, from the trinity, the incarnation, the relationship between Christ and the church, onwards. It applies here. The work of the Spirit in baptizing us into Christ, corporately as well as individually, cannot be separated from his work in baptism. The descent of the Spirit from the Father upon Jesus at his own baptism, in Matthew 3:13–17, is a case in point, demonstrating their unity and cohesion.[47]

Tom Holland takes a different line of argument. He thinks that Paul deals mainly in corporate categories rather than individual ones. Paul has referred in Romans 5 to two solidaric groups, the body of sin, human community in covenant relationship with Satan, and the body of Christ or the church.[48] In chapter 6 this corporate context continues. An individualistic focus would break Paul's line of thought. He teaches that 'believers are buried with Christ as a result of a baptism that united them to him as he was dying.' Moreover, it was a corporate baptism of an historical nature. Holland finds support for this claim also in 1 Corinthians 12:13, Galatians 3:26–9, Ephesians 4:6, and Ephesians 5:27.

In many ways, Holland has brought a necessary corrective to the dominance of individualistic thinking in the Western church. However, he unnecessarily posits a polarisation between the corporate baptism of the church into Christ and baptism itself, again thinking analytically rather than synthetically. As T.F. Torrance has argued, we are baptized *into Christ*. Christ himself was baptized; his baptism by John prospectively foreshadowed his ultimate baptism on the cross. It is into the one baptism of Christ, into participation in his death and resurrection that the Holy Spirit baptizes us, into covenantal union with Christ. This is a reality that took place historically in the death and resurrection of Christ himself, when his covenant people underwent this ordeal and deliverance in union with him. With this, due to the inseparability of spirit and matter, of sign and reality, baptism by water is indivisibly related. These are not separable realities—they are joined together, distinct but inseparable.[49]

However, Holland also makes an unfortunate disjunction between 'water baptism' and corporate baptism into Christ. In his discussion of Ephesians 4:6 he asserts 'To put water baptism into a statement which is to do with the great foundational realities that the confession declares is obviously misplaced. It cannot be claimed to have the sort of significance possessed by the eternal truths Paul has listed. If, however, the one baptism is not a reference to water, but to the one great event in which the Spirit made the Lord one with his people in the event of his vicarious atoning death, then it fits logically and naturally.'[50] The nature-grace, spirit-matter dualism here is clear. The disjunction between baptism and union with Christ is also present.[51] But these cannot be either-or matters. Jesus' parting words to the church are enough to resolve the question; the building and nurturing of his church throughout the age

'The sustained introduction of the once-for-all past historical in a context that clearly deals with what occurs actually and practically in the life-history of individuals makes inevitable the interpretation that the past historical conditions the continuously existential, not simply as laying the basis for it and as providing the analogy in the realm of the past historical for what continues to occur in the realm of our experience, but conditions the latter for the reason that something occurred in the past historical which makes necessary what is realized and exemplified in the actual life history of these same persons' (John Murray).[52]

is to be achieved first by baptism—and it is indisputable that by this he means the sacrament—and then by comprehensive teaching. The God who created heaven and earth uses material means in his saving purposes.

The clearest and most obvious reference in these passages is to the baptism common to all the people of God, of which they were and are all aware. Not surprisingly, this has been recognized down the centuries. Yet this baptism in the life-experience of the members of the church is related indissolubly to the reality that occurred in the death and resurrection of Christ, in whom all are together and corporately united. Our baptism is a participation in Christ's baptism and, for that reason, it saves us.[52]

THE MATERIAL AND THE SPIRITUAL

The two elements, the material and the spiritual, are admirably tied together by Paul in 1 Corinthians 12:13. Faced with a church influenced by a culture that despised the body and all things material—hence their questions over the resurrection (15:1–58)—Paul stresses the material means God uses to dispense his grace. Moreover, to a church riven by factions (1:10–17) he makes the point that *they all* were baptized into *one body* by the *one Spirit*, whether Jew or Greek, slave or free, and were given *one Spirit* to drink. The obvious reference is the baptism *all* would have seen and experienced—the baptism to which Paul refers in 1:13–17, where, denying that they were baptized into the name of Paul, he implies that they were all baptized into the name of the trinity (cf. Matt. 28:19), or the Lord Jesus Christ (Acts 2:38, 22:16). This same baptism is probably in view in 6:11, where he refers to their being 'washed…in the name of the Lord Jesus Christ and the Spirit of our God' at the same point as their being justified and sanctified. It is to baptism into Moses in the cloud and the sea that he comments in 10:1ff, where he urges his readers to be on their guard against temptation; they have all been baptized but so were all the Israelites and they fell into sin. So the evidence is overwhelming that the Corinthians would have understood Paul to mean that they all had been baptized into the one body of Christ, and that this was done by the Holy Spirit. The Spirit, the water and the blood go together. The Baptist theologian, G.R. Beasley-Murray affirmed that here 'we meet an explicit declaration that baptism leads into the Church' with the result of 'the incorporation of the baptized through the Spirit into the Body of Christ.'[53] As Paul could write to Titus, it was due to 'the washing of regeneration and renewal of the Holy Spirit' (Titus 3:5). On this Beasley-Murray affirms that 'no statement of the New Testament, not even John 3:5, more unambiguously represents the power of baptism to lie in the operation of the Holy Spirit.'[54]

In summary, Paul argues that we are the body of Christ, and each members of it, through the work of the Spirit. This the Spirit effects in and through baptism and all it signifies. Moreover, we are thenceforth given the Spirit to drink (1 Cor. 12:13)—a possible allusion to the eucharist.[55]

7

THE TEACHING OF
THE PROTESTANT CONFESSIONS

The Westminster Confession of Faith is the most compendious statement of Protestant and Reformed theology on record. We have already discussed much of its treatment of baptism as it unfolds it in 28:1. Now we shall summarise the rest of its presentation of the topic.

In 28:2 baptism is said to be administered by means of water in the name of the Father, the Son, and the Holy Spirit. Baptism is trinitarian. It belongs to God, not to the church, which simply administers it in the name of the holy trinity. This identifies baptism with the historic Christian church, including the church of Rome and the Orthodox.

Moreover, baptism is only to be administered 'by a minister of the Gospel, lawfully called thereunto.' This rules out baptism by midwives as practised by Rome, when the life of the newborn child was in jeopardy. It also undercuts the idea that it can be administered by any layperson. The rationale for this restriction lies in the integral connection between the Word and sacrament in Reformed theology. The sacrament is given its identity by the Word. The word of institution was necessary for a sacrament to be a sacrament. Hence, the one administering the sacrament had to be one capable of preaching the Word. Therefore, lawful calling by the church and ordination to the gospel ministry was essential to dispense the sacraments. Does this mean that someone baptized by a layperson was not validly baptized and needs to be baptized again? No, since baptism—because it is into the name of the trinity— belongs to God. Baptism by non-ordained persons, if in the triune name, is irregular but not thereby invalid.

28:3 asserts that pouring or sprinkling of water on the person baptized is the right mode of baptism. Immersion, it claims, is not necessary. However, the Assembly voted that immersion was an appropriate mode.[56]

28:5, in opposition to Rome, denies the necessity of baptism for salvation. Of course, Rome allowed the possibility of a 'baptism of desire' where a person could be saved who, for reasons outside their control, could not be baptized before their death, provided that they desired baptism. However, the divines here oppose the more representative Roman claim for baptism, as an instrumental cause of salvation, that has efficacy *ex opere operato*, by the fact of being performed. A person can be saved without having been baptized; it is not indispensable to salvation.

The Roman Catholic doctrine is challenged more directly in 28:6. Baptism is efficacious for salvation, the Confession insists. However, this is not to be understood in a temporal sense, as if at the moment of baptism the one baptized is regenerated and saved; there is no such temporal connection. Baptism is efficacious in uniting a person with Christ, regenerating and sanctifying them 'in [God's] appointed time.' Moreover, baptism is not efficacious for everyone who receives it. It is effective for God's elect, 'to such (whether of age or infants) as that grace belongeth unto.' Since the Holy Spirit makes baptism efficacious as a means of grace, it is beyond the power of the church or its ministry to do so, nor does it happen automatically.

It is in this same section that the heart of the Assembly's view of baptism appears most clearly. Allowing for the above caveats, 'the grace promised is not only offered, *but really exhibited, and conferred* [my italics], by the Holy Ghost.' It is not the case that baptism simply offers or demonstrates the grace of God, which is then received by the one baptized. Nor is it merely the fact that baptism is a visible demonstration of the gospel, setting forth washing from sins, death and resurrection to newness of life. It is, of course, both of these things. However, it is something more. The promised grace—regeneration, remission of sins, sanctification, and above all union with Christ—is *conferred* in baptism by the Holy Spirit. We have seen that this is not to be identified with the doctrine of the church of Rome. Rather, baptism unites us to Christ, regenerates, cleanses from sin, and sanctifies the elect people of God, *in God's own time*. It does so not by any power of its own but solely through the efficacy of the Holy Spirit. Moreover, the Spirit can work as and how he pleases, so baptism is not absolutely indispensable for salvation. However, anomalous situations aside, God's promises of grace in Christ are dispensed through baptism, as long as we bear in mind that the divines held that this is so in inseparable conjunction with the Word.[57] The focus of Larger Catechism 167 on improving our baptism—'all our life long'—corresponds on our side, in terms of our responsibility, to the side of divine efficacy. The Spirit works through means, in his own time, and so we are to work under his enabling throughout our life in response. As with the preaching of the Word, someone who is negligent and does not improve their baptism is placing themselves under judgment, for all God's promises and the means of grace connected to them require us to respond in faith.

For these reasons, baptism can be administered only once. Christ died once for all on the cross; his atonement can be neither repeated nor prolonged. He rose from the dead but once, never again to die. If baptism were repeatable, it would signify the incompleteness of the work of Christ, contradicting the gospel. If a person were to submit a second time to the baptismal rite only one thing could happen—he would get wet.[58]

The Reformed confessions are clear on the connection between baptism and regeneration. They consistently oppose the Roman Catholic doctrine of *ex opere operato*, which asserts that the sacraments are efficacious by the fact of their use. On the other hand, they are equally severe on those who would reduce baptism and the Lord's Supper to merely symbols.

The *Tetrapolitan Confession*, drawn up by Martin Bucer in 1530, asserts that baptism 'is the washing of regeneration, that it washes away sins and saves us.'[59] The *First Helvetic Confession* of 1536, composed by a committee consisting of Heinrich Bullinger, Grynaeus, Myconius, Jud, and Menander, assisted by Bucer and Capito, maintained that the sacraments are efficacious; they are not empty signs, but consist of the sign and the substance. 'For in baptism the water is the sign, but the substance and spiritual thing is rebirth and admission into the people of God.' All sanctifying power is to be ascribed to God alone. As for baptism '[it] is a bath of regeneration which the Lord offers and presents to his elect with a visible sign through the ministry of the Church.'[60] Both these early Reformed statements clearly allude to Titus 3:5.

A quarter of a century elapsed before the *French Confession* was drawn up in 1559, following a draft by Calvin. Chapters 34–38 refer to the sacraments. Chapter 35 states that although we are baptized only once, yet the gain that it symbolizes to us reaches over our whole lives and to our death. In chapter 37, 'in the Lord's Supper, as well as in baptism, God gives us really and in fact that which he there sets forth to us; and that consequently with these signs is given the true possession and enjoyment of that which they present to us.' The next chapter speaks of the water of baptism testifying to us in truth the inward cleansing of our souls in the blood of Jesus Christ by the efficacy of his Spirit.[61] The Confession makes a close connection between the sign and the reality; the latter is truly given with the former.

The section in the *Heidelberg Catechism* is notable.

'Q. 69: How is it signified and sealed unto thee in holy Baptism that thou hast part in the one sacrifice of Christ on the cross?

A: ...that Christ has appointed this outward washing with water, and has joined therewith this promise, that I am washed with his blood and Spirit from the pollution of my soul, that is, from all my sins, as certainly as I am washed outwardly with water whereby commonly the filthiness of the body is taken away.

Q. 70: What is it to be washed with the blood and Spirit of Christ?

A: It is to have the forgiveness of sins from God, through grace,...and also to be renewed by the Holy Ghost, and sanctified to be members of Christ...

Q. 72: Is the outward washing of water itself the washing away of sins?

A: No; for only the blood of Jesus Christ and the Holy Spirit cleanse us from all sin.

Q. 73: Why, then, doth the Holy Ghost call Baptism the washing of regeneration and the washing away of sins?

A: ...to teach us that as the filthiness of the body is taken away by water, so our sins are also taken away by the blood and Spirit of Christ...[and] by this divine pledge and token he may assure us that we are as really washed from our sins spiritually as our bodies are washed with water.[62]

Here the connection between the sign—washing with water—and the reality—cleansing from sin and regeneration—is a parallel rather than a direct conjunction.

The *Belgic Confession* (1561) points in Article 33 to the sacraments as 'visible signs and seals of an inward and invisible thing, by means whereof God worketh in us by the power of the Holy Ghost…the signs are not in vain or insignificant, so as to deceive us.' This is so since Jesus Christ is the true object presented by them, without whom they would be of no moment.[63] Article 34, on baptism, states that the sacrament 'signifies that as water washes away the filth of the body…so the blood of Christ, by the power of the Holy Ghost, internally sprinkles the soul, cleanses it from its sins, and regenerates us from children of wrath unto children of God'. Therefore the ministers administer the visible sacrament, but our Lord gives what is signified by the sacrament, the gifts and invisible grace; washing, cleansing, and purging our souls of all filth and unrighteousness; renewing our hearts and filling them with all comfort; giving unto us a true assurance of his fatherly goodness; putting on us the new man, and putting off the old man with all his deeds. Neither does baptism avail us only at the time of baptism but also through the whole course of our lives.[64]

The *Scots Confession*, composed by John Knox in 1560, Article 21, asserts that the sacraments are instituted to 'seill in their hearts the assurance of his promise, and of that most blessed conjunction, union, and societie, quhilk the elect have with their head Christ Jesus. And this we utterlie damne the vanitie of thay that affirme Sacramentes to be nathing ellis bot naked and baire signes. No, wee assuredlie beleeve that be Baptisme we ar ingrafted in Christ Jesus, to be made partakers of his justice, be quhilk our sinnes ar covered and remitted.'[65]

The *Thirty-Nine Articles of the Church of England* (1563, 1571), in Article 25—Of the Sacraments—maintains that they are not only 'badges or tokens' of Christian men's profession but 'certaine sure witnesses and effectuall signes of grace and Gods good wyll towardes vs, by the which he doth worke invisiblie in vs, and doth not only quicken, but also strengthen and confirme our fayth in hym.' According to Article 26, the unworthiness of ministers does not hinder the effect of the sacraments, since they belong to Christ. Thus baptism—Article 27—is 'a signe of regeneration or newe byrth, whereby as by an instrument, they that receaue baptisme rightly, are grafted into the Church: the promises of the forgeuenesse of sinne, and of our adoption to be the sonnes of God, by the holy ghost, are visibly signed and sealed: fayth is confyrmed: and grace increased by vertue of prayer vnto God.'

The *Second Helvetic Confession* (1562, 1566), drawn up by Bullinger and the most widely accepted of all Reformed symbols, discusses baptism in Chapter 30. Inwardly we are regenerated, purified, and renewed by God through the Holy Spirit; and outwardly we receive the assurance of the greatest gifts in the water, by which also those gifts are represented, and, as it were, set before our eyes to be behold.[66]

A later work, demonstrative of mainstream Reformed opinion shortly after the Synod of Dort, is the *Leiden Synopsis*, composed by four leading Dutch theologians in support of the Canons of Dort, and first published in 1625. Here, citing Titus 3:5, baptism is said to seal remission of sins and regeneration.[67] There is a connection between the outward sign and the washing away of sins (Rev. 1:5, 1 Cor. 6:11, Eph. 5:27, Titus 3:5), a sacramental union between the sign and the thing signified. This is a relative conjunction—the sign and the reality—and it is set before the eyes on condition of faith. Christ by his Spirit unites us with himself; no creature is capable of this. Thus God appeals both to our ears and our eyes.[68] The efficacy of baptism is not tied to the time of administration. Faith and repentance are necessary, as is love. When a seed is sown it does not germinate at the same moment; it is dependent on rain and heat. So neither the word nor the sacrament is effective at the moment of administration but at the time when the blessing of the Holy Spirit comes.[69]

The external power of baptism is as a seal. The promise, however, is joined to a condition of faith and repentance—so the grace is not sealed except to those who believe and repent. However, baptism is more than a sign and seal, for it exhibits and confers the promised reality, due to the promise of God and the life-giving Spirit.[70] It is in reality the laver of regeneration, which has perpetual efficacy.[71]

From this it is clear that the general view of evangelicals today is greatly different than that of their Protestant forebears. The classic confessions of the Reformed church all speak of the Holy Spirit conveying grace in connection with baptism, while at the same time strenuously opposing the Roman Catholic doctrine. Today it is most common to read denials that the sacraments convey grace in any form. This would meet the uninhibited opposition of a man like John Knox, who 'utterly damned' the vanity of those who thought the sacraments were only symbols. How has this change come about? There are many possible factors behind the departure from classic Protestant and Reformed teaching. One major reason has been a fear of being associated with Rome. In Britain this was probably spurred by the Oxford Movement of the nineteenth century. At that time John Henry Newman, John Keble, Edward Pusey and others led a move to reassert the centrality of the sacraments but in a very objective sense that moved close to the position of the Roman Catholic Church. In fact, Newman abandoned the Church of England for Rome in 1845. Thereafter British evangelicalism has tended to run helter-skelter in the opposite direction for fear of a similar drift. In the USA, at the same time, a large influx of immigrants from Roman Catholic countries brought about similar anxieties, provoking riots. However, in reacting out of fear in this way, we must ask whether the proverbial baby has been thrown out with the bath water?

 Baptism is related to the whole of salvation, including regeneration. Instead of avoiding this connection we should understand it Biblically and appropriately.

8

THE INDIVIDUAL

AND THE HOUSEHOLD

In chapter 4 we discussed the relationship between the individual and the corporate in both the Old Testament and New Testament. This has direct relevance to the question of who is to be baptized. In that chapter we saw that in the Bible the individual finds his or her place in the context of the community, whether it be the household, tribe or nation. Moreover, union with Christ, as the central element in the doctrine of salvation, which we discussed in the previous chapter, reinforces this paradigm. This union is to be seen in corporate terms, for being united with Christ we are simultaneously united to his church. With this as background, and with the inseparable connection between Old Testament and

New Testament in mind, we now turn to examine how the placing of the individual within the community affects our understanding of baptism.

BAPTISM AND FAITH ARE INEXTRICABLY LINKED

According to Calvin, faith is 'the principal work of the Spirit.'[72] Since Christ's work for us and in union with us is the sole basis for our justification, his righteousness alone secures our acceptance with God. This we receive only through faith because in faith 'we receive and rest on Christ alone for salvation.'[73] Moreover, faith is necessary at all stages of the Christian life, since 'we walk by faith not by sight' (2 Cor. 5:7). The Holy Spirit unites us to Christ through faith. This is so foundational to the Christian doctrine of salvation that I need say no more. It follows that baptism as the sign of union with Christ is administered in connection with saving faith. Since it is mentioned first by Jesus in his farewell discourse to the apostles before his ascension (Matt. 28:18–20), it marks the entrance into the church of all who are baptized and so is inextricably connected to saving faith.

BAPTISE CONVERTS ON PROFESSION OF FAITH

Baptism is to be administered at the point at which a person can be considered to be Christian. In the New Testament, this was on profession of faith for converts from paganism and for adult Jews. This should be the feature of baptism in any mission context anywhere in the world. There are many instances reported in Acts where, in such a missionary situation, the order is faith followed by baptism. Some of the cases were of Jews professing faith in Jesus as the Christ, in view of the transition to the new covenant and the consequent introduction of baptism. Others—in a Gentile context—were pagans who had come into contact with the gospel through the preaching of the apostles.

On the Day of Pentecost, Peter addressing a Jewish audience calls on his hearers to repent and be baptized at once, for the remission of sins and in order to receive the Holy Spirit (Acts 2:37–9). Later, when the Roman centurion Cornelius and his friends receive the Spirit while Peter preaches, Peter orders them to be baptized on the spot (Acts 10:44–8). On Paul's travels, Lydia and the jailor at Philippi are both baptized, together with their households, as they profess faith (Acts 16:14–15, 30–34).

In all these instances, baptism was given at the point at which the persons concerned could be considered to be Christian. There is no hint of any delay; the new convert was baptized at once, on the spot. The apostles were prepared to take risks. Baptism followed faith instantly. Some may argue that the apostles had special insight and so could do this without fear of the possibility of those baptized later apostatizing. This proposal is untenable; they had no special insight in these matters as the case of Simon and the many heretics who challenged the apostles proves.

WHAT OF THE CHILDREN OF BELIEVERS?

For the cumulative weight of reasons we have already mentioned, and more besides, the infant children of believers are also to be baptised and, as in the case of converts, at the point at which they can be considered Christian, as soon as possible after birth. This is due to the covenant promises of God, which include the offspring of covenant members. Behind this is the continuity of the Old Testament and New Testament in terms of the unity of the covenant of grace. It also follows from the continuance of the household as a basis of covenantal administration in the New Testament.

THE NEW COVENANT IS IN CONTINUITY WITH THE ABRAHAMIC COVENANT

Whereas credobaptists rest their case on the New Testament in isolation from the Old Testament, it is appropriate to the flow of redemptive history to see the New Covenant as fulfilling the Abrahamic covenant, and so its form in the New Testament as resting on its foreshadowing in the Old Testament. This is uniformly accepted as the overall progression of redemptive history as portrayed in the Bible. Baptism, as the initiatory sacrament of the new covenant, which fulfils all that went before, fits into this pattern in which the New rests upon the prior development in the Old. In short, we need a canonical view of baptism, as we do of any other doctrine.

In this light, baptism has been seen as the fulfilment of, and successor to, circumcision in the Abrahamic covenant. As the infant male offspring of Abraham and his seed were circumcised, so too the infant offspring of believers (Abraham's seed according to Galatians 3:23–9) are to receive the New Testament initiatory sign. If grace was given to children in the Old Testament, can it be constrained in the New Testament? Has it not rather been greatly enhanced, brought to fulfilment, and more abundantly poured out?

In a historical work, which takes recorded early church practice into consideration, David F. Wright, also rests his case on the New Testament in isolation. As a historian he looks for written evidence that particular practices occurred and, in the absence of such evidence, considers that they did not take place. This leads him to conclude that infant baptism did not occur in the New Testament since there are no particular recorded instances of an infant receiving the sign. The same methodology and its resulting argument should lead to the conclusion that monarchical episcopacy is most probably the closest form of church government associated with the apostles (as J.B. Lightfoot argued in his essay, "The Christian Ministry", published with his commentary on Philippians);[74] to the primacy of the church of Rome; to the doctrine of transubstantiation, which began to surface in the second century; and to the Pelagianism of the apostolic fathers. It would also raise questions over the practice of circumcision in the OT, since it is mentioned only at its introduction, when there is a problem (Moses' failure to circumcise his son, Exod. 4:24–6, the need to circumcise the nation due to its non-observation, Josh. 5:2–9), or in special cases to establish that the Law was followed (the circumcision of Jesus, Luke 2:21, and Timothy, Acts 16:1–3), besides incidental references to the Philistines as uncircumcised. Ironically Wright believed in the integrity and biblical provenance of infant baptism.[75]

INFANTS AND GOD'S COVENANT PROMISES

Consequently, due to the covenant promise of God the infant offspring of believers are members of Christ's church (Gen. 17:7–8). God's covenant with Abraham, now fulfilled in Christ, included the household lineage of Abraham 'throughout their generations for an ever-lasting covenant.' There is no evidence that this promise has been abrogated; if it were the covenant itself would be in question. It was uniformly accepted at the time of Jesus and the apostles and there was no indication in the New Testament writings that anything different applied. If there had been such a change, it would have provoked a huge controversy with Paul's Judaizing opponents. However, the question never appears on the agenda of these people. Moreover, in the next chapter we shall present striking and positive evidence for this conclusion from Paul himself.

THE HOUSEHOLD AND THE COVENANT

It follows that the household, integral to the life of Israel, continues as the basis of covenantal administration in the New Testament. Peter reiterates on the Day of Pentecost that the promise of God's grace is for his hearers *and their children* (Acts 2:38–9). In Acts 16 the households of both Lydia[76] and the Philippian jailor are baptized. Paul refers to his having baptized the household of Stephanus (1 Cor. 1:16). The fact that both Luke and Paul single out the household in connection with the administration of baptism indicates its continuance in covenantal administration. This is underlined in the case of the jailor since 'Acts 16:31 imposes the demand to believe on the gaoler alone, but the salvation is promised to him *and his house*.'[77]

Some argue that there is no specific mention in these passages of the presence of any infant in the households, and so the claim that they are to be baptized on the basis of what is written here is invalid. However, this argument assumes the primacy of the individual, supposing that Luke is giving a record solely of the Christian faith of particular individuals. We noted earlier that modern individualism is foreign to the world of the Bible. The relevant datum in each case is *the household*. Luke considers *the household* to be the significant unit. From this it follows that if infants were present they would, as part of the household, receive the covenant sign. The fact that particular individuals are not mentioned proves our point. The interest of the New Testament is not in the age or nature of the particular individuals who were part of the household—whether they were adults, adolescents, children or infants—but on the household as such. The propriety of infants receiving baptism is no less clear than is the baptism of other members of the households who are not specifically mentioned. We noted earlier that corporate solidarity is clear in the New Testament. There is the case of the paralytic lowered through the roof, where Jesus heals the man in connection with the faith of his friends who brought him. In James 5:13–17 the sick person is healed through the prayer of faith of the elders. The decisive thing, as Cullmann points out, is not the faith of the person healed but the faith of those who bring the invalid.[78] Behind it lies the greater realities of our natural guilt and corruption in solidarity with Adam, and our redemption in solidarity with Christ. The biblical doctrine of salvation is couched in terms of corporate solidarity. This could hardly be clearer than in the first recorded church council, debating the new development of the conversion of Gentiles. There the assembled apostles and elders heard from Peter of Cornelius' vision in which he was informed by the angel that Peter would 'declare…a message by which you will be saved, *you and all your household*' (Acts 11:14). Since the household remains the basis of administering the covenant, there is no need to mention its individual constituent members unless there is a reason pertinent to the argument of the book. The first century apostles were not operating with modern Western individualistic assumptions.[79]

GOD'S GRACE PRECEDES FAITH

This is a foundational axiom of the gospel: God's grace comes first. Throughout the Bible God's actions precede man's. God created the universe (Gen. 1:1). He did so from no previously existent matter. He brought all things into existence. He consulted no one. As he challenged Job:

Where were you when I laid the foundation of the earth? Tell me, if you have understanding. Who determined its measurements—surely you know! Or who stretched the line upon it? On what were its bases sunk, or who laid its cornerstone, when the morning stars sang together and all the sons of God shouted for joy?…Have you commanded the morning since your days began, and caused the dawn to know its place?…Where is the way to the dwelling of light, and where is the place of darkness, that you may take it to its territory and that you may discern the paths to its home? You know, for you were born then, and the number of your days is great! (Job 38:4–7, 12, 19–21).

The existence of the entire cosmos, including the human race, is owed exclusively to the creative action of the triune God.

Furthermore, the covenant of grace was not devised by Abraham. God alone initiated it. He chose Abraham, calling him from Ur, establishing his covenant with him and his offspring by sheer grace. Abraham's part was to believe God, to obey the call to leave his home and travel to the land of promise. He was purely receptive and responsive. God's grace came first; Abraham followed.[80]

Nor was the incarnation of Christ dreamt up by a group of theologians with too much time on their hands. God took the action. Before the foundation of the world, the Father determined to send the Son to save his people from their sins, the Son and the Holy Spirit inseparably and indivisibly concurring. The results that follow the incarnation—Jesus' death, resurrection and ascension to the right hand of the Father—are all due to the gracious and sovereign action of God. On our part, our faith and obedience are grounded on the atoning work of Christ as our great high priest and on the powerful action of the Holy Spirit in enabling us to believe and obey.

Since God's covenant displays first and foremost the grace of God, our part being subordinate, so baptism—as a sacrament of the covenant of grace—pre-eminently displays God's grace. From this it follows that our faith, while both necessary and of ultimate importance, is not the main thing, nor indeed the first thing. Moreover, it establishes that infants within God's covenant are appropriate subjects of baptism as their baptism rests on the grace of God expressed in his covenant promise. They are to be baptized not because they have done anything to receive it, still less to earn it, but solely due to God's gracious covenant promises. For many evangelicals, on the other hand, our faith comes first, prior to grace, and so baptism is a testimony to our own actions in faith, undertaken in obedience to God's will.

BAPTISM POINTS TO THE FUTURE

We now consider the two New Testament passages that most extensively expound baptism. A vital hermeneutical principle is to approach a topic by considering those places that most clearly refer to it.[81] In both these contexts, baptism does not follow our faith but precedes it. In Romans 6:1–9 and 1 Corinthians 10:1–13 the relationship is not between baptism and the faith that precedes but between baptism and the faith that follows. In Romans 6, Paul, answering the challenge that God's free grace gives us the license to keep on sinning asserts emphatically that this is out of the question. The reason is that we have been united with Christ in his death and resurrection. We were baptized into Christ's death, and share in his resurrection. The argument that we are to lead a godly life rests on the fact of our baptism, our baptism into Christ by the Holy Spirit to which the sacrament is directly related. The order is first baptism, then ongoing faith and obedience.

Again, in 1 Corinthians 10, Paul warns his readers against complacency. Israel had been baptized into Moses and drank Christ in the desert, yet only two of that generation entered Canaan. The reference here is to baptism as a corporate act, integral to God's covenant and the covenantal community. The implication is clear; you have all been baptized into Christ, as Paul states (1 Cor. 12:13), but you must take heed in case you too fall (v. 12). The order is the same as in Romans: first baptism, then the demand for faith and obedience. God's grace in baptism precedes our response. As Cullmann states, 'this sequence of events: act of God—response of man—is normative.'[82] This is so since baptism points to the future. Faith *after* baptism is demanded of all who are baptized, for baptism is the starting point of faith.[83]

Why should the infant offspring of a believer or believers be baptized?

- They are members of God's covenant, in which there is continuity from Old Testament to New Testament.
- The household remains the basis for covenantal administration in the New Testament.
- God's grace has priority over our response of faith. The Holy Spirit uses baptism as a means of grace.

PART THREE

CONCLUSION

In this final section we will draw together the various threads of our discussion and address some practical matters. Are the children of believers to be regarded as innocent and neutral in relation to God, as pagans, or are they to be seen as members of the visible church? The answers we give to these questions will govern the way we treat our own children. There could be few things more far-reaching for the future of the Christian faith than the spiritual nurture of the next generation.

However, there is a more significant question to ask than that—how does the New Testament view the children of believers? Did the apostles treat them in the same way as the heathen? If not, how did they view them? It is customary among evangelicals to require some kind of conversion narrative from those raised in Christian homes, akin to those given by converts from unbelief; is this true to the New Testament?

Following these questions, we will ask how such children can legitimately be denied the sacrament of baptism. In part, differences on this question emerge from comparable divergences on the nature of baptism itself. This is no arcane matter. The connection between the sacrament and the gospel it signifies and exhibits is crucial. We will bring our discussion to an end by asking some serious and pointed questions about how our answers to these questions affect our theory and practice of the church, and whether our position can be supported by the Bible.

9

CHILDREN, COVENANT,

CHURCH AND SACRAMENT

The rise of the Baptist movement coincided with the focus on the individual spawned in the Renaissance and Enlightenment. Today, the dominance of the individual in modern Western society is axiomatic. We speak of one man, one vote. Individualism is the default position of most evangelicals in Britain. However, it must be asked whether it has its roots in the post-Renaissance world and so fails to do justice to the corporate dimension of the Bible. It is a question many evangelicals have rarely, if ever, asked.

In one sense, of course, we are all credobaptists. Certainly, faith must be present in baptism, whether of a person professing faith or of a believing household of which an infant is part. However, we are using the term 'credobaptism' to refer to the claim that only those should be baptized who answer for themselves as discrete individuals.

ARE THE CHILDREN OF BELIEVERS MEMBERS OF THE CHURCH?

On credobaptist assumptions, a person becomes a member of the visible church upon profession of faith and subsequent baptism, normally in his or her teens or later. Before that, a child of a believing parent or parents cannot be considered to belong to the visible church. This is clear in statements of faith produced by such bodies as the FIEC (Fellowship of Independent Evangelical Churches) in the United Kingdom, which limit the visible church to believers:

> The universal Church is the body of which Christ is the head and to which all who are saved belong. It is made visible in local churches, which are congregations of believers who are committed to each other for the worship of God, the preaching of the Word, the administering of Baptism and the Lord's Supper; for pastoral care and discipline, and for evangelism.[84]

The Universities and Colleges Christian Fellowship (UCCF), in its Doctrinal Basis, focuses on the universal church to the exclusion of the visible church. It avoids committing itself to a doctrine of the church that might divide its constituency and is outside its specific purpose. Nevertheless, the drift of the statement seems to me to be slanted slightly towards a credobaptist doctrine of the church: 'The one holy universal church is the Body of Christ, to which all true believers belong.'[85]

Credobaptism excludes the possibility that the child is a member of the covenant, and therefore to be regarded as a Christian. Since professions of faith are necessary for baptism to take place, infants, small children and teenagers yet to take that step for themselves are not considered to be part of the universal church to which all the saved belong, which is made visible in local churches.

CREDOBAPTIST ASSUMPTIONS AND THE CHILDREN OF BELIEVING PARENTS

Given such assumptions, theoretically the child can be considered to be in one of two categories. Either the child is innocent and awaits an age of accountability, or he or she is born in Adam and so guilty of sin and, without repentance and faith, heading for eternal condemnation. In both cases, there is need for a decision at or around this notional age of accountability. The onus falls on an experience of conversion, with evidence of a major change from unbelief to faith. We will argue that both these positions are untenable.

First, we will examine the claim that a child born to believing parents is to be considered innocent, having not yet reached an age of accountability. This claim is contrary to the teaching of Scripture that all persons are born in a state of sin and moral corruption (Ps. 51:5, Eph. 2:1). Moreover, Paul writes of death spreading to the entire race due to its sharing in the sin of Adam, from which death entered the human world originally (Rom. 5:12f). Clearly, some infants die before they ever reach an age of accountability. From this it follows that they bear the consequence of Adam's sin, even if they have not had time or occasion to commit any of their own. While it is true that God is just and judges according to the case, the point remains that everyone born into this world is under the headship of Adam and participates in the guilt and moral corruption into which he plunged the race.[86] The Baptist Confession of 1689 correctly rules out claims of innocence by its view of the effects of sin.[87]

Secondly, if children born into a household with a believing parent are guilty in Adam and inherit original sin, it follows on credobaptist assumptions that they are to be treated as unbelievers requiring regeneration and repentance. If they are guilty sinners there is and can be only one way out of their predicament, through faith in Jesus Christ. It follows that parents and pastors are responsible to urge them to repent, just as they would an unbeliever or a person from an entirely pagan background. These children have no special claim on God's grace. As individuals they are accountable and guilty. We shall now consider this second alternative claim in more detail.

HOW DOES THE NEW TESTAMENT VIEW
THE CHILDREN OF BELIEVING PARENTS?

The clearest discussion of this question is given by Paul in Ephesians. In Ephesians 1:3–2:10, Paul addresses the church, informing it and its members of the great privileges they have in Christ. These run from eternity (election in Christ before the foundation of the world, foreordination to adoption as sons) through the whole gamut of history (redemption through the blood of Christ, sealing with the Holy Spirit, union with Christ so that we sit with him in heavenly places) on into the endless vistas of eternity (awaiting kindness in Christ throughout the coming ages).

Then, having sketched these immense blessings, Paul turns to consider the way church members are to fulfil their Christian responsibilities (Eph. 4:1–5:21). They are to live in a manner worthy of Christ, building one another up in the faith, following the commandments of God, being rich in good works, filled with the Holy Spirit. These things are appropriate for Christian believers. They cannot be produced by mere human effort or moral living; they are outflows of the presence and work of the Holy Spirit.

Finally, Paul addresses particular groups in the church in terms of their specific responsibilities (Eph. 5:22–6:9). Husbands are to love their wives as Christ loved the church, while wives are to submit to their husbands. Slaves are to obey their masters in the context of a Graeco-Roman culture that the church could not change overnight but would eventually transform. Part of that change was to be brought about by Christian masters acting with love, wisdom and justice to those under their authority. Fathers are to raise their children in the nurture and admonition of the Lord, with gentleness. Children are to obey their parents in the Lord.

In this section, Paul considers these children are *in the Lord* (Eph. 6:1–4). Their parents are to raise them *in the teaching of the Lord*. Their own peculiar responsibilities are to obey their parents *in the Lord*. Both believing parents and their children are *in Christ*, with mutual responsibilities befitting that status. Paul does *not* treat them as unbelievers. Nor does he suppose they are innocent; they have definite responsibilities to perform. He does not call them to repentance and faith in the way he did those he addressed in his evangelistic sermons.[88] They are *in Christ*.

Paul reinforces his instructions here by referring to the fifth commandment (Eph. 6:2–3). This was part of the Decalogue, given by Yahweh to the covenant community. Nothing could more explicitly demonstrate that he regarded these children as members of the new covenant community than that. Moreover, Paul stresses that there was a promise attached to the fifth commandment. Honouring one's parents would lead to a favourable life and a long life in the land of promise. In short, obedience *in the Lord* has as its outflow the promise of covenant blessings. The covenant law directly applied to children in the Mosaic covenant since they were members of that covenant; it continues to apply to children under the new covenant.[89]

Entailed in this is that children of believing parents also share in all the privileges all members of the church possess in Christ, just as husbands and wives, masters and slaves, and their own parent(s) do. They too were and are elect in Christ before the foundation of the world; they are also foreordained to adoption. They have been redeemed by the blood of Christ. They, as their parents, are sealed by the Holy Spirit of promise. They too are seated with Christ in heavenly places.[90] Nothing less will do justice to the force of Paul's language. To ascribe anything less to these children is to tear asunder the redemptive framework of the gospel of God's grace. Paul is talking covenantally—not even the apostle could be absolutely certain whether this or that member of his churches, adult or child, would in the end prove to be among the company of the elect. None of us are privy to such information; only God knows that. Paul writes of these children as he writes to the Christian adults. There is no difference here. Children are included and are to be regarded in the same light as adults professing faith, by virtue of the covenant of grace.

IS IT BIBLICAL TO REQUIRE A CONVERSION NARRATIVE OF CHRISTIAN CHILDREN?

Following the common assumptions and major tenets outlined earlier in the chapter, many evangelicals place an onus on those raised in believing homes to produce a narrative of conversion, in a similar way to what is asked of an adult convert from paganism. In this way they can demonstrate that they are now in a state of grace and have turned from darkness to light. However, it confronts the record that children raised in the church usually do not experience such a crisis. This is generally true from observation. Most raised in Christian homes where the faith is taught with consistency do not undergo such identifiable transitions. Obviously *some* will experience a dramatic work of the Holy Spirit—God deals with each of us differently. However, this is not normally the case, nor should there be any expectation that it will be so. Moreover, the biblical record backs this up. Of the limited biographical information given in the New Testament, Timothy had known the Scriptures from infancy (2 Tim. 3:10f.). There appears no sudden change in his status; he had evidently always been a Christian, from his very earliest years. Similarly, John the Baptist was filled with the Holy Spirit from his mother's womb (Luke 1:15, 2:39–45). You can't get much earlier than that!

So we must ask ourselves a number of questions. Is there any evidence in the New Testament that such a crisis experience was to be expected of those raised in believing homes so that they could recount a special conversion narrative? Is there a record in the New Testament of a child of believing parents having his or her baptism postponed until adulthood? Is there evidence in the New Testament that children of the faithful are called to repent and turn from their sins in the same way as an unbeliever is called to do?[91]

In summary, we must ask of evangelicals in general how coherent is their view of the status of children? They are, as Paul says, to be raised 'in the nurture and admonition of the Lord.' It is to be expected that, *given faithful teaching by parents and church*, that through the work of the Holy Spirit, they will soon confess their faith and grow in the grace and knowledge of Jesus Christ. If they belong to Christ, should we ever expect them to be relinquished, on even a temporary basis, to the world and Satan?

WHAT PLACE FOR THE SACRAMENTS?

Some argue that the church is something secondary or non-essential. This is in contrast to the Apostles creed and Nicene creed, confessed down the centuries throughout the church, Rome, Protestant, Orthodox alike. Both include integral clauses—'I believe…the holy catholic church, the communion of saints, the forgiveness of sins' in the Apostles' creed; and in the Nicene creed, 'We believe…one holy, catholic, apostolic church, one baptism for the forgiveness of sins.' These clauses refer to the church and its sacraments, summarized by baptism, which is connected to the forgiveness of sins. Those who consider the church and sacraments to be non-essential matters also run counter to the New Testament books, mostly addressed to churches. They neglect the corporate dimensions of the gospel, and forget the repeated statements of the apostles (Acts 2:38–39, 22:16, 1 Pet. 3:21, Rom. 6:1ff.) that baptism is integrally connected to the whole process of salvation. They ignore the final message of the risen Christ to the church. In this he charges it with making the nations of the world to be disciples. The first stage in this process is 'baptizing them in the name of the Father, the Son, and the Holy Spirit' (Matt. 28:19). How can this be secondary or non-essential?

Frequently, baptism has been seen as simply an act of obedience to Christ, as symbolic only. This it is but it is much more. Such an attitude is contrary to the way God operates. We saw this in our survey of the sacraments from the tree of life in Genesis onwards. As we have stressed, God created matter as well as spirit and uses material means as instruments of his grace.

John Knox thundered, in the blunt language of his day, in the *Scots Confession* (1560), "We utterlie damne the vanitie of thay that affirme Sacramentes to be nathing ellis bot naked and baire signes. No, wee assuredlie beleeve that be Baptisme we ar ingrafted in Christ Jesus, to be made partakers of his justice, be quhilk our sinnes ar covered and remitted."[92]

OUR VIEW OF THE SACRAMENTS REFLECTS OUR UNDERSTANDING OF THE GOSPEL

Years ago I heard a minister—he went on later to a very large and famous congregation—preach on Joshua 24:15, where Joshua declares 'as for me *and my household*, we shall serve the Lord.' The preacher—I shall spare his embarrassment by not naming him—repeatedly referred to the verse in these words, 'as for *me* I will serve the Lord.' This, it seemed to me then and continues to do so now, was symptomatic of a programmatic rejection of the corporate solidarity of the household. Even a passage that placarded the fact openly and explicitly before one's eyes had to be neutered so as to fit into the expectations of the context in which the preacher operated.

If we separate the individual from the household it would tend to follow that we may be inclined to a similar bifurcation between the individual and the church. Large swathes of Old Testament and New Testament teaching on the nature of the work of Christ cannot be appreciated on this individualistic basis. For Paul, man's plight and God's remedy are to be understood in corporate categories. People are either in Adam or in Christ. There are two heads of covenantal, solidaric groups. Our plight is found in one, our deliverance in the other (Rom. 5:12–21, 1 Cor. 15:12–58). The closest we may come to this in today's world is in terms of a sports team. The striker scores a goal in the final minutes; the team wins.

Moreover, an individualistic understanding of the gospel will obscure the biblical connection between salvation in Christ and the created order, the church and civil society. Spirituality becomes a state of mind and heart. It is a matter for each individual. Against this, Genesis 1:1 entails the point that all God's creation is spiritual, in that he created and maintains it, and will ultimately bring it to the end he has destined for it in Christ. Salvation is worked out in the physical world as well as the spiritual. The individual, in faith and repentance, is not acting alone. Christianity is not a case of 'me and my soul.' God's great purpose of salvation is destined to be completed in the renewal of the entire cosmos under the headship of Christ. This includes the individual—we must all trust Christ ourselves, we must all appear before the judgment seat of Christ—but it does so within a wider setting, of breathtakingly vast grandeur.

UNITY IN CHRIST

I have argued that in the New Testament baptism is connected with our union with Christ. The baptismal waters unite rather than divide. We must keep before us a commitment to the unity and catholicity of the church, one in Christ, found throughout history and throughout the world, in tandem with its holiness and apostolicity.[93] Of course, there are significant differences in the way that evangelicals understand this and in the ways baptism is administered. These are not trivial matters and, as this book has urged, they can have important consequences. We must keep in mind the need to evaluate our practice and our thinking. How far are we acting in accordance with the Bible and how far with the influences of our cultural and philosophical inheritance? My argument here is not intended to disparage the beliefs or practice – still less the Christian integrity – of those who may differ. Its purpose will be amply served if it drives us all to examine critically our own thinking for 'the supreme judge, by which all controversies of religion are to be determined, and all decrees of councils, opinions of ancient writers, doctrines of men, and private spirits, are to be examined, and in whose sentence we are to rest, can be no other but the Holy Spirit speaking in the Scripture.'[94]

How do you view the children of believers?

Is your church effectively a post-adolescent church or does it include the children of believing parents?

What biblical support do you have for your position and practice?

If you consider that Paul addresses the children of believing parent(s) in terms of their privileges and responsibilities in Christ, then should they not receive the means of grace, the covenant sign of baptism?

ENDNOTES

1 Donald Bridge and David Phypers, *The Water that Divides: Two Views on Baptism Explored* (Fearn: Christian Focus, 2008).

2 R. Letham, 'Baptism in the Writings of the Reformers,' *Scottish Bulletin of Evangelical Theology* [*SBET*] 7/2 (Autumn 1989) 21–44.

3 See also *A Faith to Confess: The Baptist Confession of Faith of 1689 Rewritten in Modern English*, 1:6 (Leeds: Carey Publications, 2005), 17.

4 See *A Faith to Confess*, 1:7.

5 R. Letham, *The Holy Trinity: In Scripture, History, Theology, and Worship* (Phillipsburg, New Jersey: Presbyterian & Reformed, 2004) 108–66.

6 Gregory Nazianzen, *Oration 31*, 21, J.P. Migne, ed. *Patrologia cursus completus series Graeca* [*PG*], 36:156–57.

7 Ibid., 3, *PG* 36:136–37.

8 Ibid., 21–24, *PG* 36:156–60.

9 Ibid., 23, *PG* 36:157–60.

10 B. B. Warfield, *The Westminster Assembly and Its Work* (New York: Oxford University Press, 1934) 226–7.

11 A. v. Harnack, *Marcion: The Gospel of an Alien God* (J. E. Steely; Durham, North Carolina: The Labyrinth Press, 1990); Irenaeus, *Against Heresies* (*Ante-Nicene Fathers of the Christian Church* [*ANF*] 1:315–578; Theophilus, *Against Marcion* (Lost); Tertullian, *Against Marcion* (*ANF*

3:271–474; Hippolytus, *Against Marcion* (Lost); 'Muratorian Fragment,' *Documents Illustrative of the History of the Church* (B. Kidd; London: SPCK, 1938) 1:166–8.

12   *The Westminster Confession of Faith* [*WCF*] 7:5–6.

13   The 1689 Baptist Confession states: 'This covenant is revealed in the gospel; first of all to Adam in the promise of salvation by 'the seed of the woman', and afterwards, step by step, until the full revelation of salvation was completed in the New Testament.' *A Faith to Confess,* 7:3.

14   See P. E. Hughes, *Paul's Second Epistle to the Corinthians: The English Text, with Introduction, Exposition and Notes* (London: Marshall, Morgan & Scott, 1961) 103–5; R. Letham, *The Work of Christ* (Leicester: Inter-Varsity Press, 1993) 44–6; P. R. Jones, 'The Apostle Paul: Second Moses to the New Covenant Community,' *God's Inerrant Word: An International Symposium on the Trustworthiness of Scripture* (ed. J. W. Montgomery; Minneapolis: Bethany Fellowship, 1974) 219–41.

15   R. Letham, *The Work of Christ,* 177–80; R. Letham, *Union with Christ: In Scripture, History and Theology* (Phillipsburg, New Jersey: Presbyterian & Reformed, 2011) chapter 4.

16   R. Letham, *The Holy Trinity: In Scripture, History, Theology, and Worship* (Phillipsburg, New Jersey: Presbyterian & Reformed, 2004) 59–60.

17   A. R. Cross, 'Baptism in the Theology of John Calvin and Karl Barth,' *Calvin, Barth and Reformed Theology* (N. B. MacDonald; Eugene, Oregon: Wipf & Stock, 2008) 82–3.

18   Ibid., 80.

19   See R. Letham, *The Work of Christ* (Leicester: Inter-Varsity Press, 1993).

20   See R. Letham, 'Is Evangelicalism Christian?' *Evangelical Quarterly* 67/1 (1995) 3–33.

21   G. Bray, *The Doctrine of God* (Leicester: Inter-Varsity Press, 1993) 158.

22   See my argument on this point in R. Letham, *The Holy Trinity: In Scripture, History, Theology, and Worship* (Phillipsburg, New Jersey: Presbyterian & Reformed, 2004) 59–60.

23   Cyprian, *On the Unity of the Catholic Church* 4, in *ANF* 5:422.

24   Augustine, *Enchiridion* 65, in *Nicene and Post-Nicene Fathers of*

the Christian Church, First Series 3:258.

25   J. Calvin, *Institutes* 4:1:4.

26   T. Ware, *The Orthodox Church* (London: Penguin Books, 1969) 283–4.

27   *Catechism of the Catholic Church* (London: Geoffrey Chapman, 1994) 1240.

28   *The First and Second Prayer Books of Edward VI* (London: Dent, 1968) 398.

29   R. Letham, *The Westminster Assembly: Reading Its Theology in Historical Context* (Phillipsburg, New Jersey: Presbyterian & Reformed, 2009) 339–43.

30   R. Letham, 'Baptism in the Writings of the Reformers,' *SBET* 7/2 (Autumn 1989) 21–44; H. O. Old, *The Shaping of the Reformed Baptismal Rite in the Sixteenth Century* (Grand Rapids: Eerdmans, 1992) 264–82; J. C. McLelland, *The Visible Words of God: An Exposition of the Sacramental Theology of Peter Martyr Vermigli 1500–62* (Edinburgh: Oliver and Boyd, 1957) 140; M. Bucer, *In Epistolam D. Pauli Ad Romanos* (Basel, 1562) 321; J. Calvin, *Institutes* 4:15:19; P. M. Vermigli, *In Epistolam S. Pauli Apostoli Ad Romanos Commentarii Doctissimi* (Basel: Petrum Pernam, 1558) 199.

31   See R. Letham, *The Holy Trinity: In Scripture, History, Theology, and Worship* (Phillipsburg, New Jersey: Presbyterian & Reformed, 2004) 59–60 for a discussion of the new covenant name of God.

32   '*Washing (loutron)* is almost certainly a reference to water baptism. All the early church fathers took it this way.' John Stott, *The Message of 1 Timothy and Titus: The Life of the Local Church* (Leicester: Inter-Varsity Press, 1996), 204. In footnote 20, Stott points to 1 Cor. 6:11 and Eph. 5:26 in support; *Ibid.* See also Calvin's comment: 'I have no doubt that there is at least an allusion here to baptism and, I have no objection to the explanation of the whole passage in terms of baptism.' Eds. David W. Torrance and Thomas F. Torrance; Trans., T.A. Smail, *Calvin's Commentaries: The Second Epistle of Paul to the Corinthians and the Epistles to Timothy, Titus, and Philemon* (Grand Rapids: Eerdmans, 1964), 382. I am indebted to The Rev. Todd Matocha for directing me to these references.

33 See Bo Reicke, *The Disobedient Spirits and Christian Baptism* (Copenhagen: Acta Seminaii Neotestamentici Upsaliensis, 1946); W.J. Dalton, S.J., *Christ's Proclamation to the Spirits: A Study of 1 Peter 3:18–4:6* (Rome: Pontifical Biblical Institute, 1965); J.N.D. Kelly, *A Commentary on the Epistles of Peter and Jude* (London: A.&C. Black, 1969), 150–164; W. Grudem, *The First Epistle of Peter: An Introduction and Commentary* (Leicester: Inter-Varsity Press, 1988), 203–239.

34 See Luke 12:49–50.

35 Brian Gerrish uses this terminology in his discussion of Calvin's view of the Lord's Supper; see B. Gerrish, *Grace and Gratitude: The Eucharistic Theology of John Calvin* (Minneapolis: Fortress Press, 1993). He concludes that Calvin holds to the latter position.

36 A. N. Lane, *Justification by Faith in Catholic-Protestant Dialogue: An Evangelical Assessment* (London: T.&T. Clark, 2002) 186–7.

37 *WCF* 28:1. See also *A Faith to Confess*, 29:1.

38 Augustine, *On the Gospel of John*, 80:3, in *NPNF,* First Series, 7:344.

39 *WCF* 28:3.

40 Letham, *Westminster Assembly*, 332–3, 346–7.

41 *Catechism of the Catholic Church* (London: Geoffrey Chapman, 1994) 1128, 1256–7, 1261.

42 *WCF* 28:6.

43 A. R. Cross, 'Baptism in the Theology of John Calvin and Karl Barth,' *Calvin, Barth and Reformed Theology* (N. B. MacDonald; Eugene, Oregon: Wipf & Stock, 2008) 80.

44 D. M. Lloyd-Jones, *The Church and the Last Things* (London: Hodder & Stoughton, 1997) 44; D. M. Lloyd-Jones, *Romans: An Exposition of Chapter 6 The New Man* (London: The Banner of Truth Trust, 1972) 30–7; T. Holland, *Contours of Pauline Theology: A Radical New Survey of the Influences on Paul's Biblical Writings* (Fearn: Mentor, 2004) 141–9.

45 D. Lloyd-Jones, *Romans 6*, 31.

46 Ibid., 36.

47 G. Beasley-Murray, *Baptism in the New Testament* (Exeter: Paternoster Press, 1972).

48 Holland, *Contours*, 137.

49 'The One Baptism Common to Christ and his Church,' in T. F. Torrance, *Theology in Reconciliation* (Grand Rapids: Eerdmans, 1975) 82–105.

50 Holland, *Contours*, 148.

51 See my book R. Letham, *Union with Christ: In Scripture, History and Theology* (Phillipsburg, New Jersey: Presbyterian & Reformed, 2011).

52 See the connection between the redemptive-historical and the personal-existential elements of union with Christ in Romans 6 drawn by John Murray, 'Definitive Sanctification,' *Calvin Theological Journal*, 2 (1967):5–21; H.M. Ridderbos, *Paul: An Outline of his Theology* (Grand Rapids: Eerdmans, 1975), 406–410; and Richard B. Gaffin, Jr., *The Centrality of the Resurrection: A Study in Paul's Soteriology* (Grand Rapids: Baker, 1978), 53–58.

53 G. Beasley-Murray, *Baptism in the New Testament* (Exeter: Paternoster Press, 1972) 169–70.

54 Beasley-Murray, *Baptism*, 215. John Stott supports this claim—see note 32.

56 Immersion has always been practised by the Greek Orthodox Church—and the Greeks know a thing or two about their own language. *The Catechism of the Catholic Church* indicates that the meaning of the verb *baptidzo* is 'to immerse' while *The Book of Common Prayer of the Church of England* (1552) states that the infant is to be 'dipped' in water. So credobaptists are not the only ones who maintain that immersion is the appropriate mode of baptism.

57 This is not the theology of baptism commonly held today in conservative Protestant circles, or even in many Reformed and Presbyterian churches. Yet so integral to Reformed theology was its sacramentalism that claims to being Reformed must be challenged that lack this vital element.

58 This is so since baptism is ultimately something God does. Moreover, there is no necessary temporal relationship between baptism and faith, since the latter can precede or follow the former. In the last analysis, the one baptized receives the sacrament in connection with faith, whether his or her own or that of the believing household.

59   A. C. Cochrane, *Reformed Confessions of the 16th Century* (London: SCM, 1966) 74.

60   Cochrane, *Reformed Confessions*, 107–8.

61   Cochrane, *Reformed Confessions*, 156–7.

62   P. Schaff, *The Creeds of Christendom* (Grand Rapids: Baker, 1966) 3:329–31.

63   Cochrane, *Reformed Confessions*, 213.

64   Cochrane, *Reformed Confessions*, 214.

65   Schaff, *Creeds*, 3:467–70.

66   Cochrane, *Reformed Confessions*, 282.

67   J. Polyander, *Synopsis Purioris Theologiae, Disputationibus Quinquaginta Duabus Comprehensa* (Leiden: Ex officina Elzeverianus, 1625) 644–7.

68   Polyander, *Synopsis Purioris Theologiae*, 648–9.

69   Polyander, *Synopsis Purioris Theologiae*, 651.

70   Polyander, *Synopsis Purioris Theologiae*, 652.

71   Polyander, *Synopsis Purioris Theologiae*, 653–4.

72   J. Calvin, *Institute*, 3:1:1.

73   *WCF* 14:1–2; *A Faith to Confess*, 14:1–2.

74   J. Lightfoot, *Saint Paul's Epistle to the Philippians* (London: Macmillan, 1881) 186–202.

75   D. F. Wright, *Infant Baptism in Historical Perspective: Collected Studies* (Milton Keynes: Paternoster, 2007).

76   Since Lydia was apparently a single business woman, it is probable that her household servants are included in the reference.

77   O. Cullmann, *Baptism in the New Testament* (Studies in Biblical Theology; London: SCM, 1950) 53.

78   Ibid., 55.

79   By the same token one could argue that there is no mention in the New Testament of women receiving the Lord's Supper. Nor is there any New Testament reference to a child of believing parents having his or her baptism postponed until adulthood. Ultimately, such arguments rest on the assumption that only express statements of the Bible constitute authoritative revelation. If that were so, and good and necessary deductions eliminated from consideration, virtually every

doctrine of the Christian faith would be destroyed. We discussed this point in chapter 1.

80 Genesis 11:31–12:4, Joshua 24:1–5.

81 *A Faith to Confess*, 1:9.

82 Cullmann, *Baptism*, 49.

83 Ibid., 50–4.

84 See http://www.fiec.org.uk/AboutUs/Beliefs/tabid/509/Default. aspx, accessed 25 March 2011.

85 See http://www.uccf.org.uk/about-us/doctrinal-basis.htm, accessed 20 May 2011.

86 See J. Murray, *The Imputation of Adam's Sin* (Grand Rapids: Eerdmans, 1959).

87 *A Faith to Confess*, 6:1–5.

88 This does *not* mean that they are *not* to be called to repentance and faith. All in the church are to believe and repent on an ongoing basis, as part of the progressive path of sanctification to which all in Christ are called. The point is that Paul does not treat these children as unbelievers but as part of the church, as members of God's covenant, in the same way as he regards the others at Ephesus.

89 I am grateful to The Rev. Dr. S. E. ('Woody') Lauer for this important observation.

90 Eph. 1:3–2:7.

91 These questions at least negate the opposing question about the absence of a specific New Testament reference to the baptism of an infant.

92 P. Schaff, *The Creeds of Christendom* (Grand Rapids: Baker, 1966) 3:467–70.

93 See the Niceno-Constantinopolitan creed, 'We believe one holy, catholic, apostolic church.' Robert Letham, 'Catholicity Global and Historical: Constantinople, Westminster, and the Church in the Twenty-First Century,' *The Westminster Theological Journal* 72 (2010):43–57.

94 *WCF* 1:10; See also *A Faith to Confess*, 1:10.

BIBLIOGRAPHY

A Faith to Confess: The Baptist Confession of 1689 Rewritten in Modern English. Leeds: Carey Publications, 2005.

Augustine. *Enchiridion*.

———. *Tractates on the Gospel of John*.

Beasley-Murray, G.R. *Baptism in the New Testament*. Exeter: Paternoster Press, 1972.

Bray, Gerald. *The Doctrine of God*. Leicester: Inter-Varsity Press, 1993.

Bridge, Donald and David Phypers. *The Water that Divides: Two Views on Baptism Explored*. Fearn: Christian Focus, 2008.

Bucer, Martin. *In epistolam D. Pauli ad Romanos*. Basel, 1562.

Calvin, John. *Institutes of the Christian Religion*. 2 vols. Philadelphia: Westminster Press, 1960.

———. *Calvin's Commentaries: The Second Epistle of Paul to the Corinthians and the Epistles to Timothy, Titus, and Philemon.* Eds. David W. Torrance and Thomas F. Torrance. Trans., T.A. Smail. Grand Rapids: Eerdmans, 1964).

Catechism of the Catholic Church. London: Geoffrey Chapman, 1994.

Cochrane, A.C. *Reformed Confessions of the 16th Century.* London: SCM, 1966.

Cross, Anthony R. 'Baptism in the Theology of John Calvin and Karl Barth.' In *Calvin, Barth and Reformed Theology*, Neil B. MacDonald, 57–87. Eugene, Oregon: Wipf & Stock, 2008.

Cullmann, Oscar. *Baptism in the New Testament.* Studies in Biblical Theology. London: SCM, 1950.

Cyprian. *On the Unity of the Catholic Church.*

Dalton, W.J. *Christ's Proclamation to the Spirits: A Study of 1 Peter 3:18–4:6.* Rome: Pontifical Biblical Institute, 1965.

Gaffin, Richard B. Jr. *The Centrality of the Resurrection: A Study in Paul's Soteriology.* Grand Rapids: Baker, 1978.

Gerrish, B. A. *Grace and Gratitude: The Eucharistic Theology of John Calvin.* Minneapolis: Fortress Press, 1993.

Gregory of Nazianzus. *Oration 31.*

Grudem. W. *The First Epistle of Peter: An Introduction and Commentary.* Leicester: Inter-Varsity Press, 1988.

Harnack, Adolf von. *Marcion: The Gospel of an Alien*

God. trans. John E. Steely. Durham, North Carolina: The Labyrinth Press, 1990.

Hippolytus. *Against Marcion*. Lost.

Holland, Tom. *Contours of Pauline Theology: A Radical New Survey of the Influences On Paul's Biblical Writings*. Fearn: Mentor, 2004.

Hughes, Philip Edgcumbe. *Paul's Second Epistle to the Corinthians: The English Text, with Introduction, Exposition and Notes*. London: Marshall, Morgan & Scott, 1961.

Irenaeus. *Against Heresies*.

Jones, Peter R. 'The Apostle Paul: Second Moses to the New Covenant Community.' In *God's Inerrant Word: An International Symposium on the Trustworthiness of Scripture*, edited by John Warwick Montgomery, 219–41. Minneapolis: Bethany Fellowship, 1974.

Kelly, J.N.D. *A Commentary on the Epistles of Peter and Jude*. London: A&C Black, 1969.

Lane, A. N. S. *Justification by Faith in Catholic–Protestant Dialogue: An Evangelical Assessment*. London: T.&T. Clark, 2002.

Letham, Robert. *The Holy Trinity: In Scripture, History, Theology, and Worship*. Phillipsburg, New Jersey: Presbyterian & Reformed, 2004.

———. *Union with Christ: In Scripture, History and Theology*. Phillipsburg, New Jersey: Presbyterian & Reformed, 2011.

————. *The Work of Christ*. Leicester: Inter-Varsity Press, 1993.

————. 'Baptism in the Writings of the Reformers,' *Scottish Bulletin of Evangelical Theology* 7/2 (Autumn 1989): 21–44.

————. *The Westminster Assembly: Reading Its Theology in Historical Context*. Phillipsburg, New Jersey: Presbyterian & Reformed, 2009.

————. 'Catholicity Global and Historical: Constantinople, Westminster, and the Church in the Twenty-First Century,' *Westminster Theological Journal* 72 (2010): 43-57.

Lightfoot, J.B. *Saint Paul's Epistle to the Philippians*. London: Macmillan, 1881.

Lloyd-Jones, D.M. *Romans: An Exposition of Chapter 6 The New Man*. London: Banner of Truth Trust, 1972.

————. *The Church and the Last Things*. London: Hodder & Stoughton, 1997.

McLelland, J. C. *The Visible Words of God: An Exposition of the Sacramental Theology of Peter Martyr Vermigli 1500–62*. Edinburgh: Oliver and Boyd, 1957.

'Muratorian Fragment.' In *Documents Illustrative of the History of the Church*, Edited by B.J. Kidd, 1:166–68. London: SPCK, 1938.

Murray, John. *The Imputation of Adam's Sin*. Grand Rapids: Eerdmans, 1959.

————. 'Definitive Sanctification.' *Calvin Theological Journal* 2 (1967): 5–21.

Old, Hughes Oliphant. *The Shaping of the Reformed Baptismal Rite in the Sixteenth Century.* Grand Rapids: Eerdmans, 1992.

Polyander, Johannes, et. al. *Synopsis purioris theologiae, Disputationibus quinquaginta duabus comprehensa.* Leiden: ex officina Elzeverianus, 1625.

The First and Second Prayer Books of Edward VI. London: Dent, 1968.

Reicke, Bo. *The Disobedient Spirits and Christian Baptism.* Copenhagen: Acta Seminarii Neotestamentici Upsaliensis, 1946.

Ridderbos, H.M. *Paul: An Outline of his Theology.* Grand Rapids: Eerdmans, 1975.

Schaff, Philip, ed. *The Creeds of Christendom.* 3 vols. Grand Rapids: Baker, 1966.

Stott, John. *The Message of 1 Timothy and Titus: The Life of the Local Church.* Leicester: Inter-Varsity Press, 1996.

Tertullian. *Against Marcion.*

Theophilus. *Against Marcion.* Lost.

Torrance, Thomas F. *Theology in Reconciliation.* Grand Rapids: Eerdmans, 1975.

Vermigli, Pietro Martire. *In epistolam S. Pauli apostoli ad Romanos commentarii doctissimi.* Basel: Petrum Pernam, 1558.

Ware, Timothy. *The Orthodox Church.* London: Penguin Books, 1969.

Warfield, Benjamin B. *The Westminster Assembly and its Work.* New York: Oxford University Press, 1934.

Westminster Confession of Faith.

Wright, David F. *Infant Baptism in Historical Perspective: Collected Studies.* Milton Keynes: Paternoster, 2007.